CHANGE YOUR BRAIN, CHANGE YOUR BODY

COOKBOOK

Eat Right to Live Longer, Look Younger, Be Thinner, and Decrease Your Risk of Obesity, Depression, Alzheimer's Disease, Heart Disease, Cancer, and Diabetes

TANA AMEN, BSN

DANIEL G. AMEN, MD

Published by MindWorks Press, Newport Beach, California.

A Division of Amen Clinics, Inc.

www.amenclinics.com

Authors: Daniel G. Amen, MD & Tana Amen, BSN

Photographer: Vince Weathermon

Layout and Design: Jaclyn Frattali

Other Books and Programs By Dr. Daniel Amen

CHANGE YOUR BRAIN, CHANGE YOUR BODY, Harmony Books, 2010

MAGNIFICENT MIND AT ANY AGE, Harmony Books, 2009, New York Times Bestseller

THE BRAIN IN LOVE, Harmony Books, 2007

MAKING A GOOD BRAIN GREAT, Harmony Books, 2005, Amazon Book of the Year

PREVENTING ALZHEIMER'S, with neurologist William R. Shankle, MD, Putnam, 2004

HEALING ANXIETY AND DEPRESSION, with Lisa Routh, MD, Putnam, 2003

NEW SKILLS FOR FRAZZLED PARENTS, MindWorks Press, 2003

IMAGES OF HUMAN BEHAVIOR: A Brain SPECT Atlas, MindWorks Press, 2003

HEALING THE HARDWARE OF THE SOUL, Free Press, 2002

HEALING ADD, Putnam, 2001

HOW TO GET OUT OF YOUR OWN WAY, MindWorks Press, 2000

CHANGE YOUR BRAIN, CHANGE YOUR LIFE, Three Rivers Press, 1999, New York Times Bestseller

ADD IN INTIMATE RELATIONSHIPS, MindWorks Press, 1997

Would You Give 2 MINUTES A DAY For A Lifetime Of Love, St. Martin's Press, 1996

A CHILD'S GUIDE TO ADD, MindWorks Press, 1996

A TEENAGER'S GUIDE TO ADD, with Antony Amen and Sharon Johnson, MindWorks Press, 1995

MINDCOACH: Teaching Kids To Think Positive And Feel Good, MindWorks Press, 1994

THE MOST IMPORTANT THING IN LIFE I LEARNED FROM A PENGUIN, MindWorks Press, 1994

TEN STEPS TO BUILDING VALUES WITHIN CHILDREN, MindWorks Press, 1994

THE SECRETS OF SUCCESSFUL STUDENTS, MindWorks Press, 1994

HEALING THE CHAOS WITHIN, MindWorks Press, 1993

Printed in China

Dedication

To Chloe

TABLE OF CONTENTS

FOREWORD

Daniel G. Amen, MD

I have been looking for this book my entire life. I have been looking for guidance on how to eat that is rational, thoughtful, comprehensive, health promoting, and delicious. In the pages of this cookbook you will find wonderful recipes, ideas, and tips to get control of your brain and your body.

Who knew that eating right would cause a joyful explosion of taste and leave you feeling satisfied! Many people think that eating right is boring and monotonous. If you follow the recipes in this cookbook you will find your diet filled with nutritious and delicious meals that you will want again and again. I remember the first time I tried the sweet potato soup (page 58) I asked Tana if we could have it every week. Then there was the turkey chili (page 104) and I had the same reaction, as I did with the spaghetti squash pasta (page 101) and the avocado ahi tuna (page 120), the lentil soup (page 67), and the spinach barley soup (page 61). It just goes on an on.

I am proud to introduce my wife to the world through her talent of putting together amazing and healthful meal plans. Tana is a gifted mother and health promotion nurse.

Bill Cosby once wrote, "I am what I ate … and I'm frightened." The food you eat can destroy your health or be your best medicine.

The Amen Clinics 7 Rules for Brain Healthy Eating

> **Rule #1**
>
> **Think high-quality calories in versus high-quality energy out.**

Don't let anyone tell you that calories don't count. They absolutely do. But it is not as simple as calories in versus calories out. I want you to think about eating mostly high-quality calories. One cinnamon roll can cost you 720 calories and will drain your brain; while a 400-calorie salad made of spinach, salmon, blueberries, apples, walnuts, and red bell peppers will supercharge your energy and make you smarter.

The research about calories is very clear. If you eat more calories than you need, you will be fatter, sicker, and less productive. In the famous rhesus monkey study, researchers followed a large group of monkeys for 20 years. One group ate all the food they wanted; the other group ate 30 percent less. The monkeys who ate anything they wanted were three times more likely to suffer from cancer, heart disease, and diabetes, plus researchers saw significant shrinkage in the important decision-making areas of their brains.

You need to know how many calories a day you need to either maintain or lose weight. These calculators are included on our website at www.amenclinics.com/cybcyb. The average active 50-year-old man needs about 2,200 calories a day to maintain his weight, while most women need about 1,800 calories. To lose a pound a week, you need to eat 500 calories a day less than you need.

You also need to KNOW how many calories a day you actually put in your body, just like you need to know how much money you spend. Overeating is the exact same thing as overspending. When you overeat you bankrupt your brain and your body.

If weight is a problem for you keep a journal just like you keep a checkbook. Start the day with the number of calories you can spend and have a sense of where you are throughout the day. This strategy made a huge difference for me. When I actually wrote down everything I ate for a month it caused me to stop lying to myself about my calories. I have created the *Change Your Brain, Change Your Body Daily Journal* to help you keep track of your calories and other brain healthy habits.

At the Amen Clinics, we are conducting one of the largest studies on retired NFL players, and many of them are obese when they first come to see us. One of the players in our NFL study wrote that when he started counting his calories it opened up a new world of self-abuse that he was completely unaware of.

Rule #2

Drink plenty of water and not too many of your calories.

Did you know that your brain is 80 percent water? Anything that dehydrates it, such as too much caffeine or much alcohol, decreases your thinking and impairs your judgment. Make sure you get plenty of water every day.

On a recent trip to New York City, I saw a poster that read, "Are You Pouring On The Pounds? Don't Drink Yourself Fat." I thought it was brilliant. A recent study found that on average Americans drink 450 calories a day, twice as many as we did 30 years ago. Just adding the extra 225 calories a day will put 23 pounds of fat a year on your body and most people tend to NOT count the calories they drink.

Did you know that some coffee drinks or some cocktails, such as margaritas, can cost you more than 700 calories? One very simple strategy that can help you lose a lot of weight is to eliminate most of the calories you drink.

My favorite drink is water mixed with a little lemon juice and a little bit of the natural sweetener stevia. It tastes like lemonade, so I feel like I'm spoiling myself and it has virtually no calories. You will find other brain healthy drinks included in this cookbook.

Rule #3

Eat high-quality lean protein throughout the day.

High-quality lean protein will help balance your blood sugar and provides the necessary building blocks for brain health. Keeping your blood sugar balanced throughout the day by eating some protein with every meal and snack is key to curbing cravings and boosting brain performance. Great sources of protein include fish, skinless turkey or chicken, beans, raw nuts, and high-protein vegetables, such as broccoli and spinach. Did you know that spinach is nearly 50 percent protein? I use it instead of lettuce on my sandwiches for a huge nutrition boost.

Rule #4

Eat low-glycemic, high-fiber carbohydrates.

This means eat carbohydrates that DO NOT spike your blood sugar. Spikes in your blood sugar are typically followed by a crash about 30 minutes later that leaves you feeling sluggish and spacey. Look for carbohydrates that are also high in fiber, such as those found in whole grains, vegetables, and fruits, like blueberries and apples.

When it comes to weight loss and brain function, carbohydrates are not the enemy. They are essential to your life. Bad carbohydrates are the enemy. These are carbohydrates that have been robbed of any nutritional value, such as simple sugars (cookies, cakes, and brownies) and refined carbohydrates (muffins, cinnamon rolls, and white bread). If you want to live without cravings, eliminate these completely from your diet. I like the old saying, "the whiter the bread the faster you are dead."

Sugar is not your friend. Sugar increases inflammation in your body, increases erratic brain cell firing, and has been recently implicated in aggression. In a new study, children who were given sugar every day had a significantly higher risk for violence later in life. I don't agree with the people who say everything in moderation; cocaine or arsenic in moderation is not a good idea. The less sugar in your life the better your life will be.

Rule #5

Focus your diet on healthy fats.

Eliminate bad fats, such as all trans fats and most animal fat. Did you know that fat stores toxic materials? So when you eat animal fat, you are also eating anything toxic the animal ate. Yuk. Did you know that certain fats that are found in pizza, ice cream, and cheeseburgers fool the brain into ignoring the signals that you should be full? No wonder I used to always eat two bowls of ice cream and eight slices of pizza.

Focus your diet on healthy fats, especially those that contain omega-3 fatty acids, found in foods like salmon, avocados, walnuts, and green leafy vegetables.

High cholesterol levels are not good for your brain. A new study reports that people who had high cholesterol levels in their 40s had a higher risk of getting Alzheimer's disease in their 60s and 70s. The B vitamin niacin has very good scientific evidence it helps lower cholesterol. Avocados and garlic can help as well.

But don't let your cholesterol levels go too low. Did you know that low cholesterol levels have been associated with both homicide and suicide? If I am at a party and someone is bragging to me about their low cholesterol levels, I am always *very* nice to that person.

Rule #6
Eat from the rainbow.

This means put natural foods in your diet of many different colors, such as blueberries, pomegranates, yellow squash, and red bell peppers. This will boost the antioxidant levels in your body and help keep your brain young. Of course, this does not mean Skittles or jelly beans.

Rule #7
Cook with brain healthy herbs and spices to boost your brain.

Herbs and spices can do much more than just enhance the flavor of your food. Many have been used throughout history for medicinal purposes, and modern-day researchers agree that they can be good medicine. For example, did you know that some of the everyday spices in your kitchen cupboard can help protect you from Alzheimer's disease and depression and can improve your memory and attention? See more about this in Chapter 2 Using Brain Healthy Herbs and Spices.

Eating in a brain healthy way is about abundance, not deprivation. It is about great taste and wise spending. Your attitude here is critical. If you think of it as a loss of lasagna you will not stick with it. But, when you think of eating right as a GAIN in energy, a GAIN in longevity, a GAIN in brain power, and a GAIN in time with your loved ones, you are much more likely to stay on track.

50 BEST BRAIN FOODS

Almonds, raw

Almond milk, unsweetened

Apples

Asparagus

Avocados

Bananas

Beans (black, pinto, garbanzo)

Bell peppers (yellow, green, red, orange)

Beets

Blackberries

Blueberries

Broccoli

Brussels sprouts

Carrots

Cheese, low fat

Cherries

Chicken, skinless

Cranberries

Egg whites, DHA enriched

Grapefruit

Herring

Honeydew

Kiwi

Lemons

Lentils

Limes

Oats

Olives

Olive oil

Oranges

Peaches

Peas

Plums

Pomegranates

Raspberries

Red grapes

Soybeans

Spinach

Strawberries

Tea, green

Tofu

Tomatoes

Tuna

Turkey, skinless

Walnuts

Water

Whole wheat

Wild salmon

Yams & Sweet Potatoes

Yogurt, unsweetened

MORE ON BRAIN HEALTHY NUTRITION

You can find more great information about how to eat the brain healthy way on the Change Your Brain, Change Your Body website at www.amenclinics.com/cybcyb. Among the many tools available, you will find:

Free Change Your Brain, Change Your Body Questionnaire: This questionnaire is a great start to helping you evaluate the health and well-being of your brain and body. It can help you determine your brain type so you can take a targeted, individualized approach to help you get and keep the body you have always wanted.

Free Calorie Calculator: Find out how many calories you should be eating based on your height, weight, gender, age, and activity level.

Free BMI Calculator: Knowing your body mass index (BMI) gives you a good sense if you're at a healthy weight.

Free Brain Healthy Shopping List: Print out this list of more than 100 brain healthy foods and take it with you to the grocery store to make sure you stock up on the great brain foods.

Free Plans for the 5 Types of Overeaters: Based on our brain-imaging work, I have identified five types of overeaters. Here you will find what works and doesn't work for each type.

Free 100 Ways to Leave Your Blubber: 100 easy ways to cut calories and slim down.

Free Quiz: Is Your Behavior Killing You?: Medical experts have identified the 12 most common preventable causes of death. Find out how many of these modifiable health risks you have.

CHAPTER 1
Eat Right to Think Right
& Tips for Success

CHAPTER 1
EAT RIGHT TO THINK RIGHT & TIPS FOR SUCCESS

With a better brain comes a better body. And so much more! One of the most important pillars of having a better brain is nutrition. With proper nutrition comes better energy, focus, health, relationships, and yes… a better body. Without proper nutrition comes fatigue, mental fog, hyperactivity, distractibility, irritability, poor sleep, increased risk for many health and mental health disorders, and more.

Your brain uses 20-30 percent of the calories you consume, and feeding it right is essential to being able to think, focus, and make intelligent decisions. What you eat day to day is either helping or hurting your brain and your body. Food can be poison to your system or it can be your best medicine. It would be great if we had a little monitor, like a watch, that registered the quality of everything we ate. You would be able to see that every time you eat sugar you create inflammation in your system and that whenever you are not eating enough vegetables or are eating too much saturated fat, your arteries are getting clogged.

We don't have that, but our bodies are sensitive, sophisticated machines. They are capable of telling us everything we need to know. Unfortunately, much of what we eat and our lifestyles desensitize us to these signals. Additionally, we have learned to stop listening to our bodies as a result of social cues, commercials, and advertisements. We need to get back in tune with our bodies. The book *Change Your Brain, Change Your Body* gives some great information about becoming more aware of your body.

For many years most people who know me would agree that I was the epitome of health and fitness. I danced in school, modeled, and began seriously working out at the age of 17. But as I painfully discovered, "fitness" is not synonymous with "health." I grew up in an environment of anti-nutrition. I was raised by a single working mother and often had to fend for myself.

As a child, my favorite breakfast was Lucky Charms. Lunch was usually warm tortillas drowning in butter and caked with enough sugar to soak up the butter. If someone was around to cook, it was usually some kind of greasy pan-fried steak with mashed potatoes and gravy… and don't forget the ice cream.

When I was 25 years old I was diagnosed with thyroid cancer. After being diagnosed with cancer I became more of a fitness fanatic. Even so, I struggled with cancer several more times, had high cholesterol, high triglycerides, had my gall bladder removed, and had a hormone imbalance. Related to the thyroid cancer, I also had a significant struggle with depression. Even at my best, I usually drank at least a pot of coffee every day to maintain the energy level I expected to play at. The rollercoaster ride was vicious.

On the exterior I was the essence of fitness, so why was my health less than optimal? These questions led me on my personal quest to understanding health. As I began dissecting my lifestyle and doing my own research, I discovered that for all my good intentions, some of the things I was doing to enhance my fitness were actually impairing my health. It was evident, as my body was the manifestation of this simple truth.

When I discovered that fitness does not equal health, I decided *to get healthy*. My journey began in nursing school where I obtained a BSN, a Bachelor of Science in Nursing. Additionally, the college I attended was strictly vegetarian and focused on the care of the whole person. I spent years working as a neurosurgical intensive care nurse, learning how important brain function really is to everyday behavior. And then… put together a neurosurgical ICU nurse and a neuropsychiatrist who spends his days looking at people's brains, and brain health is usually a daily topic of dinnertime conversation. Often our six-year-old joins in at the dinner table with a game we developed called "Is This Good For My Brain, Or Bad For My Brain?"

As a mother and a wife, I am a very busy person. We entertain frequently and are committed to living an active, fitness-focused lifestyle. With all these balls to juggle, it wouldn't be easy to make nutrition a primary focus, *unless I planned!* Planning ahead makes it so much easier to eat right.

Most of the recipes included in this cookbook are very simple and quick. They are designed to be healthy, easy, and things your children will eat. Be patient with your children if they have been used to eating fast food every night. Don't force the change, but remember that "exposure equals preference." Continue to expose them to nutritious choices and limit the number of unhealthy choices available.

Remember that the healthiest options are always those that take the least amount of preparation and processing. If I could convince everyone to eat a primarily plant-based diet of raw vegetables, fresh vegetable juice, nuts, fruit, and limited animal protein, there would be little need for cookbooks. But food is a big part of our lives. People often use food as the focus to gather and commune, to show appreciation and love. We cook as a hobby, and we love to eat. Cooking is an expression of creativity.

While I have tried to include enough healthy recipes to keep meals interesting, the reality is, you should try to limit the amount of "concentrated" foods you eat. Concentrated foods are foods that don't come from a plant-based source or that are cooked and processed to the point that most of the nutritional value has been stripped away. Instead, opt for as many raw and lightly cooked choices as possible. My favorite recipes are the salads and the vegetable dishes.

Throughout this cookbook, you may come across a few ingredients that are new to you. When you learn what they can do for your brain and body, you will want to add them to your shopping list.

Following are some tips to help you set up your kitchen, help you stay on track when you are away from home, and to help you plan ahead. You are more likely to be successful if you have a plan and get into a rhythm.

Eat More Veggies, Less Animal Protein

In general, I recommend that you try to make 70 percent of your daily food consumption come from raw, or lightly cooked, plant-based sources. Remember though, that based on your individual brain type, you may benefit from eating a higher-protein, lower-carbohydrate diet. Through his brain imaging work, my husband has identified five types of overeaters based on brain types. You can determine your brain type by taking the Change Your Brain, Change Your Body Questionnaire online at www.amenclinics.com/cybcyb.

In our home we eat a heavily plant-based diet that is light in animal protein. Personally, I limit animal protein to deep-sea fish—such as wild salmon, ahi, albacore, mahi mahi and sea bass— once or twice a week. I understand that this is still not a mainstream way of eating, and I respect those of you who prefer some animal protein in your diet. Because of this, you will find that many of the vegetarian recipes include a meat option. Similarly, for those of you who do not eat animal protein, I have included vegetarian options for many of the meat-based recipes. Often, I cook a vegetarian meal and make a side of fish that can be added for the rest of the family or guests. However, I find that when I serve a tasty and nutritious vegetarian meal, most people don't miss the meat at all.

For those of you, like my husband, who choose to eat animal protein, choose wisely. Brain healthy sources of animal protein include wild salmon, tuna, herring, skinless chicken and turkey, and DHA-enriched eggs. For meats, it is best to choose grass-fed, free-range, hormone-free, and antibiotic-free products.

The Myth That Vegetarians Don't Get Enough Protein

There is an ongoing debate about which mammals are the strongest pound for pound. But the gorilla is generally considered the strongest land mammal in the world, with the ability to lift 10 times its body weight. With the exception of the miniscule amount of protein consumed when they preen one another, gorillas are vegetarians. Elephants and horses are other examples of incredibly strong mammals that eat plant-based diets.

Probably the greatest myth about the vegetarian diet is that it is lacking in protein. It can potentially be lacking in protein if you are not conscious of a well-balanced diet. However, many plant-based foods have far more protein than most people realize and as long as you are eating a *well-rounded* diet there is little need to worry about a lack of protein. For example, are you aware that broccoli is more than 40 percent protein, spirulina is 70 percent protein, spinach is 50 percent protein, and certain nuts are 20 percent protein? See the following chart for the amount of protein in many plant-based foods.

Additionally, many cuts of meat are not as healthy as you may think in regards to protein intake. Many cuts of meat are higher in saturated fat than you may realize. By the time meat is cooked, much of the protein is denatured. While I am not attempting to sway anyone away from a carnivorous diet, "lack of protein" should not be the reason to hold on to this plan.

If you feel the need to increase your protein intake, you may consider a protein powder supplement. I rarely use protein supplements, but if I do I use rice protein. Soy protein powders should not be used in high quantities because they contain too much estrogen. Whey protein is another option that is derived from cow's milk. Since I personally do not consume milk protein any longer, I typically do not use whey protein. For those of you who prefer whey protein, which is considered one of the highest sources of pure protein, Designs For Health is my favorite provider.

Some people notice that they truly feel great when they consume a diet consisting of lean animal protein. Make the determination based on reality not on myths. If you eat a well-balanced vegetarian, conscious diet, and you are well informed, you will not be lacking in protein. Also make this determination based on objective data, such as your important health numbers. (You can find out more about the important health numbers you need to know in *Change Your Brain, Change Your Body* and the *Change Your Brain, Change Your Body Daily Journal*.) Pay attention to how these dietary changes affect your energy and vitality *as well as your body chemistry*.

Don't get too hung up on the term "alkalize." Basically, it means eat more vegetables — the less processed the better. Raw is best. Hydrate your body with water, and lots of it!

Protein Percentages in Plant-Based Foods

Soybean sprouts	54% protein
Spinach	49% protein
Broccoli	45% protein
Kale	45% protein
Mung bean sprouts	43% protein
Cauliflower	40% protein
Bamboo shoots	39% protein
Mushrooms	38% protein
Lettuce	34% protein
Chinese cabbage	34% protein
Wheat germ	31% protein
Zucchini	28% protein
Navy beans	26% protein
Cabbage	22% protein
Pumpkin seeds	21% protein
Whole wheat	17% protein
Lemons	16% protein
Oats	15% protein
Walnuts	13% protein
Honeydew melon	10% protein
Strawberries	8% protein
Oranges	8% protein
Cherries	8% protein
Apricots	8% protein
Watermelon	8% protein
Grapes	8% protein
Brown rice	8% protein
Filberts	8% protein
Pecans	5% protein

Source: Nutritive Value of American Foods in Common Units, USDA Handbook No. 456

Alkalize, Alkalize, Alkalize!!!

Don't get too hung up on the term "alkalize." Basically, it means eat more vegetables — the less processed the better. Raw is best. Hydrate your body with water, and lots of it! Raw nuts (not roasted) are great. "Alkalinizing diets" are a current trend. I'm not really an advocate of any type of diet, especially when they start making life complicated and become really restrictive. But I do believe in common sense.

Let me explain the basics of these alkalinizing diets. For those of you who have not taken basic chemistry, a pH scale shows how acid or alkaline a substance is. The scale goes from 0-14, with 7 being neutral. Starting at 7 and going down to 1 the scale measures more and more acidic (a strong acid such as battery acid is 0.3). Going up from 7 substances become more alkaline (the pH of ammonia is about 11.6). Water is usually around 7.

Why is this important to you? We live in an acid-producing society. Most of the foods we have become accustomed to consuming are acidic by nature, and not all that healthy if not consumed in moderation. Sugar, alcohol, coffee, saturated fats, and excessive animal protein are bad for our health if consumed in excess. But why? One of the main reasons is because they acidify your system, which causes inflammation, excessive phlegm, constipation, and undue stress on our system.

Raw vegetables, some fruit (in moderation), whole and sprouted grains, raw nuts, deep-sea fish, and lots of water have the opposite effect. These foods are alkaline by nature. They decrease inflammation, cleanse, and they are loaded with antioxidants. If you don't believe me, try it. Notice the difference in your energy when you eat acidifying foods compared to when you alkalize! It is remarkable.

10 Tips To Stay On Track Anywhere, Anytime

1. Always pack your lunch. Always, always, have a small ice chest ready to go. It should consist of: a bottle of green water, a bottle of lemon water, a bag of fresh-cut vegetables, and a bag of raw soaked almonds. Consider a dip for your veggies (maybe some hummus, salsa, almond butter, or guacamole). I always have a fresh salad or some sort of quinoa salad, and possibly a veggie sandwich or a piece of fruit, depending on how long I will be gone.

2. If I know I'm going somewhere that there will be "temptation," I take something sweet like coconut milk yogurt or fruit salad…. or I make a fresh sorbet.

3. Always keep fresh avocados handy for guacamole. I mash fresh avocados and use it as a dip for my other fresh vegetables (instead of using bread I dip fresh veggies).

4. Always keep hummus, baba ghanoush and salsa available in the refrigerator for dipping vegetables.

5. Keep raw almonds with you in a Ziploc bag. Consider keeping some soaked almonds in the refrigerator. They are great and very satisfying when they are soft. They are a tasty snack.

How Much Water Should You Be Drinking and What Kind?

"How much" is an easy question to answer. "What kind" sounds a little funny. Let me elaborate. The formula for how much water you should drink is:

Take your body weight in pounds divided by 2. Whatever number you get is the amount you should drink, in ounces. For example: I weigh 120 pounds. 120 divided by 2 is 60. I need to drink at least 60 ounces of water every day. This does not include tea or other beverages. *This is the amount of water I drink.* However, it does include water with lemon or greens added to it.

Now for the second part of the question: What kind of water should you be drinking?

"Green water" is an alternative to fresh vegetable juice. While there is no replacement for fresh vegetable juice, there are times when fresh juice is not convenient. And let's face it, some people just don't like the taste of wheat grass. My six-year-old simply will not drink fresh wheat grass… yet! But she drinks "green water" regularly. And she likes it.

Green water is a form of dehydrated or freeze-dried (freeze-dried is healthier) vegetables. Just add one scoop to 16 ounces of water. I usually use 24-32 ounces of water with one scoop since I enjoy having more than one in a day. Most of these mixes have an extensive list of vegetables and a very high ORAC value. ORAC is a method of measuring antioxidant capacities—the higher the number, the better. A scoop of "green mix" added to your water is typically the equivalent of about five servings of vegetables. Greens can be found in almost any health food store and stores such as Whole Foods.

Greens come in several flavors. The plain flavor actually tastes pretty good. However, if you just can't get used to the "grassy" taste try adding a few drops of orange, lemon, or vanilla crème stevia (more on stevia later). My daughter's favorite is the chocolate flavor. There is no sugar, only a little unsweetened, pure cocoa. I add a couple drops of chocolate raspberry stevia and voila! It tastes like a rich chocolate drink, minus the sugar, fat, and calories. My daughter isn't allowed to have soda at home. This is her idea of a "sweet drink."

The advantages of drinking green water are numerous. First, it alkalizes and detoxifies your system. Second, it adds substance to your water and can be pretty filling. It often helps curb hunger and between-meal snacking. It keeps you drinking! It tastes good so you tend to drink more water. You should still have some plain water during the day, but since most people don't drink as much water as they should this is a healthy, tasty way to increase your water intake. It is also convenient when traveling. It is not always easy to find juice bars when traveling, but "greens" come in travel packs.

When giving up addictions like coffee and other tough habits to break, wheat grass and green water can work wonders. Many times having something to replace the habit with is part of the battle. Additionally, replacing the habit with a more "alkaline" choice will reduce your body's craving for the addiction. I experienced this first hand and have heard many people say the same. Many people claim that drinking wheat grass and green water even helps to prevent headaches when eliminating caffeine.

When I wanted to quit drinking coffee, I began going to the local juice bar instead of the local coffee shop. My favorite juice is "Goddess of Greens" (wheat grass, cucumber, kale, celery, and parsley). This is one of the healthiest things I can think of for your body and your brain, but apparently it's an acquired taste. I love them. My husband and daughter think I'm drinking "goat juice"… since goats eat grass.

A daily shot of wheat grass is one of the greatest gifts you can give your body. One ounce of wheat grass has 20 amino acids, 91 minerals, and is 70 percent chlorophyll. The chlorophyll molecule is virtually identical to the hemoglobin molecule in blood. Wheat grass provides a tremendous amount of energy.

Lemon water is another great option. Lemon makes water tasty, alkalinizing, and cleansing. To really count you need more than just a little slice, as served in restaurants. Although it would seem that lemon water should be acidic (because of the citric acid), it actually has the opposite effect on the system. That is because lemons have very little sugar. It is the sugar that is the problem.

Change Your Condiments

Satisfy Your Sweet Tooth With Stevia

My best health food find by far is stevia. Stevia is not sugar and is not a chemically processed sugar substitute. It is extracted from the stevia leaf and is completely natural. It does not affect blood sugar levels the way sugar does and it does not acidify the system the way toxic sugar substitutes do. Stevia has been shown to have many health benefits, including stabilizing blood sugar levels and helping reduce blood pressure. Many of the recipes I've included use stevia as the sweetener of choice.

A word of caution: use stevia sparingly until you get the hang of it. It is much sweeter than sugar and requires a fraction of the amount. If you use too much it has a bitter taste. For many things I prefer vanilla-flavored stevia. For some reason the vanilla-flavored stevia doesn't seem to have the same bitter taste if you accidentally use a few drops too many.

Instead of butter or margarine, I use Earth Balance as a healthy alternative. Butter is an animal protein and essentially all fat and cholesterol. Margarine is processed and a poor substitute. Earth Balance is a "buttery spread" made from an expeller pressed oil blend. It has a great flavor, melts easily, and is easy to cook with. However, it still has a high fat content and, as with all spreads and dressings, it should be used sparingly.

Simple Swap: Vegenaise Instead of Mayonnaise

Vegenaise is an egg-free mayonnaise alternative made with grape seed oil. It isn't processed with the same chemical processing and tastes great. If you need a mayonnaise spread for sandwiches, this (or some other natural alternative) is a good choice. However, my personal favorite for spreading on sandwiches or wraps is a thin layer of avocado or hummus. This allows the natural taste of the vegetables and grains to come through and is much healthier.

Try Almond Butter

Replace peanut butter with crunchy, raw almond butter. Peanut butter is not really very healthy. This was a great disappointment for me to discover. Peanuts are actually a legume, and they are highly susceptible to contamination during growth and storage, which can lead to infection by the mold fungus, *aspergillus flavus*, releasing the toxin, *aflotoxin* (a potent carcinogen). Almond butter is a much better choice. Try spreading it on your veggies or fruit for a tasty, nutritious snack.

> ### All About Cooking Oils

There is a huge controversy brewing over which oil is the best to use for cooking. Traditionally, many recipes call for olive oil for sautéing and baking. It is said that olive oil is only stable up to 200 degrees F. At high temperatures, or when the oil begins to smoke, olive oil and many other oils break down and can actually become toxic. At best they lose any nutritional

10 Tips To Stay On Track Anywhere, Anytime

6. If you're on the run try toasting a slice of whole grain bread (preferably Ezekiel) and spreading mashed avocado on it. This is a great alternative to cheese or lunch-meat.

7. Keep yummy leftovers in the refrigerator. When we cook, I make sure there are plenty of leftover vegetables, grains, and salad for the following day. I usually pack it in lunch-size containers right then so I'm ready to go.

8. Keep a bottle or bag of dry stevia with you. I always keep a bottle of my favorite flavor of stevia with me in my purse. Artificial sweeteners are poison!

value they had. Safflower, sunflower, and sesame oil are good choices for many recipes. For frying, broiling, deep frying, or anything requiring high heat better alternatives are clarified butter or ghee

11 (the one time I recommend butter), or coconut oil. Personally, I prefer using refined coconut oil for cooking on the rare occasion that I need oil.

In any case I would recommend organic, unrefined, and expeller pressed oils. The processing of oils strips them of all nutritional value, leaving them nothing more than liquid fat. Oils naturally have the flavor and color of whatever nut or vegetable they came from. Processing and petrochemical solvents lead to light-colored, neutral-flavored oils. Unrefined oils are usually found in most health food stores.

In most cases you don't need to use oil for sautéing at all! You will notice that most of the recipes in this cookbook give the option of using a little vegetable broth for sautéing instead of oil. Try it and see if you notice a difference.

Many nutrients and vitamins require the use of some fat for absorption. This does not mean that you need to use cooking oil. However, using a little Udo's oil or olive oil in your salad as dressing, or topping certain dishes with avocado or almonds can be tasty and healthful. Your body not only digests these fats easily, but you will get more nutritional value from what you eat in most cases. Just be aware that just because a little is good, it does not mean that more is better. Like all things, moderation is key. For those of you who are not familiar with Udo's oil, it is a buttery-tasting blend of oils including flax, sunflower, sesame, and evening primrose as well as rice and oat germ.

Go Organic!

Many people wonder why organic produce and other groceries are preferable. They are usually passed over as the more expensive choice. So what is the real value? Nonorganic produce are sprayed with pesticides and grown in chemically enhanced fertilizers that can be toxic. Meats are injected with hormones. While it has been determined that the amount of pesticide residue on produce is inconsequential to our health, the concern is for the cumulative effect over time.

When cooking with vegetables, such as carrots, potatoes, yams, cucumbers, or apples, consider leaving the skin on. Peeling the skin greatly reduces the nutritional value. Just below the skin is where the highest concentration of vitamins and minerals are. However, if you are not purchasing organic produce be sure to peel the skin, as the skin also holds the toxic chemicals.

Eat Live, Water-Rich Food

Our bodies are 70 percent water. We derive our energy from live, water-rich foods like vegetables and fruits. Your goal should be to derive 70 percent of your daily intake from raw or lightly cooked vegetables, fruits, and water-rich foods; 30 percent of your intake or less should come from concentrated foods. Concentrated foods are foods that lose their nutritional value during the cooking process, such as meats, breads, and dairy. Many of the recipes in this cookbook are simple salads, juices, and lightly cooked or raw meals.

Non-Dairy Milk Options

Many people have trouble digesting dairy products. Why? Less than 40 percent of humans produce the enzyme lactase to be able to digest milk after the age of two. To say that we are "lactose intolerant" is actually a misconception. It would be more accurate to call those few who can easily digest cow's milk "lactose tolerant." Because of this, most of the recipes in this book use non-dairy substitutes for milk.

Almond milk is a personal favorite of mine. It is used in most of the recipes. However, you may certainly substitute it with soy or rice milk. One of the reasons I prefer almond milk is because it comes unsweetened and because I just like the flavor better. It doesn't have the aftertaste that soy milk has, and it doesn't contain any estrogen, which is found in soy milk.

On the list of the 50 best brain foods, you will find unsweetened yogurt. If you have trouble digesting dairy, try coconut milk yogurt or rice yogurt instead. Coconut milk yogurt is delicious. It has live cultures and is very tasty. Rice yogurt has lower fat content, but has a slight aftertaste. In either case, remember that these should be consumed sparingly as they contain sugar.

It is a misconception that dairy products build strong bones in humans. Milk products contain lactose, which is sugar. Sugar is acidic and may cause inflammation, ultimately burdening the entire system and, yes the bones. Does this mean that you should never drink milk or any milk products? No, but be careful with them. If you consume dairy products be sure that you are not lactose intolerant and that your body has the capability of breaking down lactase. Also, be sure to follow the guidelines for consuming more "live, water-rich foods" and increase your water intake. Count dairy products into the 30 percent of daily "concentrated foods." Dairy products do not count as "live" or "water-rich" foods.

10 Tips To Stay On Track Anywhere, Anytime

9. Know where the healthy restaurants and stores are in your area. I always know where I can stop for lunch or a quick snack in a pinch. Worst case, I know I can stop at a grocery store and buy a red bell pepper, almonds, and an avocado. It doesn't take any longer than going through a drive-thru at a fast food restaurant.

10. Stop and get a shot of wheat grass as often as possible. When possible get a drink consisting of a variety of fresh green juices. Your energy will be greatly enhanced. It is no more expensive than a "super frappawhoopa, machachocolato espresso with a cherry on top," but it is a whole lot healthier!

CHAPTER 2
Using Brain Healthy Herbs & Spices

CHAPTER 2

USING BRAIN HEALTHY HERBS & SPICES

Herbs and spices do so much more than just add flavor to nutritious foods. They can also do wonders for your brain. Enhanced memory, protection from depression, and increased attention are just some of the benefits. Look for the Brain Boosters boxes on the recipe pages for dishes that use these brain healthy herbs and spices.

Saffron: In addition to adding a wonderful flavor to rice, soups, and other dishes, saffron also wards off depression and improves memory and the ability to learn. Some scientific studies have found this tasty spice to be as effective as antidepressant medication. In terms of learning, several studies suggest that saffron enhances learning and may be useful for the treatment of memory impairment.

Curry: This popular Indian spice is actually a combination of many different spices, including turmeric, which contains a chemical called curcumin that has shown promise in the prevention and treatment of Alzheimer's disease, Parkinson's disease, and strokes. A potent antioxidant, curcumin reduces inflammation and helps prevent the formation of plaques in the brain that are associated with the disease and can break up these plaques.

Oregano: Oregano is one of the most potent antioxidants known to man. Oregano protects cells in the body and brain from free radicals that cause premature aging. Oregano is also a source of omega-3 fatty acids, which enhance brain function and offer protection from depression and PMS symptoms. Herbalists suggest that it may also be helpful for insomnia and the relief of migraine headaches.

Cinnamon: If you want to improve your working memory or your ability to pay attention, try chewing some cinnamon gum or just taking a whiff of some cinnamon tea. Research shows that the scent of cinnamon is enough to enhance these functions. In addition, cinnamon helps regulate blood sugar levels, which improves impulse control so you are less likely to give in to cravings for cookies, cakes, and candy.

Garlic: Compounds in this kitchen staple cause blood vessels to relax and dilate, increasing blood flow to the brain, which results in better brain function. This is one of the reasons scientists suggest that eating garlic regularly can help reduce the risk of strokes and improve heart health. Adding cloves of fresh garlic to your meals can also boost your immune system so you and your family can fight off cold and flu bugs.

Ginger: That tangy treat commonly served with sushi may have powerful anti-aging properties that will help keep your brain young. Some studies have found that ginger reduces oxidative stress (that is what causes cells to age and eventually die) in brain tissue. Not only that, ginger also acts as an anti-inflammatory, which may offer protection from neurodegenerative diseases.

Thyme: This flavorful spice often used in soups and stews increases the amount of an important type of fat called DHA in the brain. DHA protects neurons from premature aging.

Sage: Having trouble remembering all the ingredients in your favorite brain healthy recipes? Try adding more sage. It has been found to boost memory in healthy people of all ages and can improve mental functioning in people with Alzheimer's disease.

Basil: This potent antioxidant improves blood flow to the brain that enhances overall brain function. It also boasts anti-inflammatory properties that offer protection from Alzheimer's disease.

Rosemary: The antioxidant and anti-inflammatory properties in this spice may offer protection from the cognitive decline associated with dementia and may provide new hope in the treatment of Parkinson's disease.

CHAPTER 3

Focus & Energy Breakfast Recipes

Breakfast is one of the most important meals of the day.
Starting the day right is critical to balancing your blood sugar
and boosting your brain. Here are recipes we use in the Amen
household that will give you a good start.

◆ **2 Servings** ◆ **133 Calories** ◆ **8 Brain Boosters**

Ingredients:

Egg Beaters or egg whites (equivalent of 4 eggs)
Vegetarian option: Use firm tofu (equivalent of 4 eggs) or about 8 ounces tofu
2 teaspoons ghee or coconut oil
½ cup asparagus tips
¼ cup red onion, finely chopped
2 handfuls spinach leaves
1 vine-ripened tomato, thinly sliced
2 garlic cloves, finely chopped
1 teaspoon fresh rosemary, chopped
1 teaspoon fresh thyme, chopped
1 tablespoon fresh basil, chopped
Real Salt to taste
Pepper to taste

Optional: Dried spices may be substituted. However, for the health benefit as well as flavor, you should try to use fresh herbs. If using dried herbs, use no more than 1 teaspoon of each.

Preparation:

1. Whisk Egg Beaters or egg whites in a bowl and set aside.
2. In a small nonstick pan, heat 1 teaspoon ghee or oil over medium heat. Sauté onion and asparagus for about 2 minutes, until softened. Add garlic and sauté for another 2 minutes.
3. Remove onion, asparagus, and garlic from pan. Place on dish and set aside.
4. Add 1 teaspoon ghee or oil to pan. Pour egg mixture into pan. As egg mixture begins to set, add onion, asparagus, and garlic mixture to eggs, but do not scramble. Allow mixture to set in nice round shape.
5. Add rosemary, thyme, basil, spinach, salt, and pepper.
6. Place frittata on plates and top with tomato slices.

Optional: If substituting egg product with tofu follow same steps above but use tofu in step 4. Crumble tofu and cook until slightly browned. Continue with steps 5 and 6. The "frittata" will not have the same set look that eggs do, but the flavor will be delicious.

You will notice that this recipe and many others call for "Real Salt." I love this brand of salt, which is pure, has no additives, chemicals, or heat processing. It is healthier for you than regular table salt.

BRAIN BOOSTERS
50 best brain foods: asparagus, spinach, tomato, eggs (or tofu)
Brain healthy spices: garlic, rosemary, thyme, basil

Nutrition Per Serving

133 Calories	15 g Protein
12 g Carbohydrates	4 g Fat
2 g Saturated Fat	0 mg Cholesterol
258 mg Sodium	2 g Fiber

ALMOND BUTTER QUINOA

BREAKFAST

♦ **4 Servings** ♦ **205 Calories** ♦ **4 Brain Boosters**

Ingredients:

1 cup quinoa, rinsed

2 cups almond milk (or rice milk), unsweetened

2 tablespoons chunky almond butter

¼ teaspoon cinnamon

¼ teaspoon maple extract

1 banana, thinly sliced

2 tablespoons slivered almonds

Optional: ¼ cup raisins

Optional: 1 packet dry stevia

Add any other brain healthy fresh fruit topping of your choice.

Preparation:

1. In a medium saucepan, over high heat, bring milk, quinoa, almond butter, cinnamon, and maple extract to a boil.
2. Reduce heat, cover and simmer until milk is absorbed, about 15 minutes.
3. Turn off heat and add raisins. Let stand for 5 minutes.
4. Add banana and almonds. Add stevia, if desired.
5. Serve warm.

BRAIN BOOSTERS

50 best brain foods: unsweetened almond milk, bananas, almonds

Brain healthy spices: cinnamon

Nutrition Per Serving

205 Calories	7 g Protein
32 g Carbohydrates	9 g Fat
0 g Saturated Fat	0 mg Cholesterol
99 mg Sodium	4 g Fiber

♦ **2 Servings** ♦ **171 Calories** ♦ **6 Brain Boosters**

Ingredients:

Egg Beaters (equivalent of 4 eggs) or egg whites
Vegetarian option: Use 7 ounces firm or extra firm tofu
2 teaspoons ghee or refined coconut oil
1 cup mixed vegetables, chopped
(be creative—use broccoli, red bell peppers, chives, garlic, spinach, or any other veggies you love)
2-3 avocado slices
¼ cup salsa (preferably fresh)
2 Ezekiel sprouted grain tortillas

Preparation:

1. Melt ghee or oil in skillet over medium heat. Add vegetables and sauté until slightly tender, about 2-3 minutes. Do not overcook. Vegetables are more nutritious and flavorful when they are not cooked through. If using spinach, do not add until the very last minute. Spinach is best when barely cooked.

2. Add Egg Beaters, egg whites, or other egg substitute. If using tofu, crumble with your hands and add to pan for about 3 minutes. Stir until cooked through. Egg product should be firm and no longer opaque (no liquid). Remove from heat.

3. If preferred, tortillas may be warmed in a pan or over burner briefly.

4. Divide egg mixture evenly between the two tortillas. Place mixture in the center of the tortillas. Use salt and pepper as desired.

5. Add sliced avocado to each tortilla.

6. Add salsa as desired.

7. Fold bottom of tortilla up ¼ of the length of the tortilla (this keeps the eggs from falling out of the bottom). Fold one side over and roll.

If taking on the go, wrap with wax paper to keep from falling apart.

BRAIN BOOSTERS
50 best brain foods: eggs (or tofu), broccoli, red bell pepper, spinach, avocado
Brain healthy spices: garlic

Nutrition Per Serving	
171 Calories	9 g Protein
21 g Carbohydrates	7 g Fat
2 g Saturated Fat	0 mg Cholesterol
359 mg Sodium	5 g Fiber

♦ **2 Servings** ♦ **273 Calories** ♦ **4 Brain Boosters**

Ingredients:

1 head celery
2 cucumbers (peel the cucumber if you choose, but most of the nutritional value is just beneath the surface of the skin)
½ cup broccoli, cut off as much of the stem as possible
½ cup parsley, rinsed
½ head kale
1 handful spinach
2 tablespoons fresh mint
1 avocado

*Optional: 1 scoop Amazing Greens
or other freeze-dried vegetable blend*

Optional: ½-1 scoop vanilla whey or soy protein powder

Optional: 1 packet stevia to remove tart taste of broccoli and cucumber skin

Optional: Be creative and add what ever other vegetables you love.

It doesn't get any healthier than this. This is one of my favorite breakfast meals. It is filling and contains the perfect combination of fresh green vegetables, healthy fats, and protein. You will need a juicer for this recipe.

Preparation:

1. Blend celery, cucumber, broccoli, parsley, and kale in juicer.
2. Pour juice into blender. Add spinach, mint, avocado, and Amazing Greens powder.
3. Blend until smooth.
4. Add protein powder and stevia last. Blend for no more than 10 seconds. Blending protein powder too long breaks down the protein.
5. Pour and serve.

BRAIN BOOSTERS
50 best brain foods: broccoli, spinach, avocado
Brain healthy spices: cinnamon

GOING GREEN: *For those of you who have never "gone green" or cleansed before, the taste may take some getting used to. I promise if you give it a try you will become addicted. Imagine every cell in your body being bathed in pure nutrition and charged with energy. You will feel so good that you will be begging for more!*

Nutrition Per Serving

273 Calories	9 g Protein
33 g Carbohydrates	15 g Fat
2 g Saturated Fat	0 mg Cholesterol
171 mg Sodium	13 g Fiber

BREAKFAST

BRAIN BERRY MUESLI

◆ **2 Servings** ◆ **294 Calories** ◆ **7 Brain Boosters**

Ingredients:

½ cup old-fashioned rolled oats
(do not use instant oats)
1 cup water
1 tablespoon cranberry juice,
unsweetened
2 teaspoons honey (may
substitute half with a few drops
of stevia)
1 tablespoon raw almonds,
chopped
1 tablespoon raw sunflower
seeds
2 tablespoons dried cranberries
1 tablespoon wheat germ
½ teaspoon vanilla
1 large apple, grated
1 banana
¼ cup fresh blueberries
½ cup almond milk,
unsweetened

*Optional: ½ cup plain or vanilla-
flavored coconut milk yogurt (this
is non-dairy with live cultures)*

Advance Preparation:

Oats, almonds, and sunflower seeds need to soak overnight. In a large bowl combine oats, water, cranberry juice, honey, almonds, sunflower seeds, cranberries, wheat germ, and vanilla. Cover and refrigerate overnight. Soaking the nuts and oats initiates the sprouting process, making the muesli a living meal filled with natural energy.

Preparation:

1. Remove the soaked mixture from refrigerator.
2. Grate the apple and add to mixture.
3. Slice banana and add to mixture.
4. Place into serving bowls.
5. Sprinkle blueberries on top.
6. Add milk or coconut milk yogurt and serve.

Optional: Skip the milk and put a scoop of plain or vanilla-flavored coconut milk yogurt (this is non-dairy but has live cultures and is absolutely delicious) on top instead for added protein and flavor.

BRAIN BOOSTERS
50 best brain foods: oats, water, raw almonds, apples, bananas, blueberries, unsweetened almond milk

Nutrition Per Serving	
294 Calories	6 g Protein
66 g Carbohydrates	7 g Fat
1 g Saturated Fat	0 mg Cholesterol
43 mg Sodium	9 g Fiber

BANANA NUT OATCAKES

♦ **4 Servings** ♦ **275 Calories** ♦ **3 Brain Boosters** ♦ **Gluten-Free**

Ingredients:

2 cups rolled oats

2 tablespoons walnuts

1 cup almond milk, unsweetened

2 tablespoons oat or brown rice
flour (you may use wheat flour
if you choose)

1 tablespoon lecithin liquid

1 teaspoon vanilla

½ teaspoon Real Salt

1 tablespoon agave syrup

1 banana, thinly sliced

These are calorie-dense and very filling, but they are high-quality calories. You should not have to eat many of them before you feel pleasantly satisfied.

Preparation:

1. Put oats in a blender and set on "chop" or "grind." Blend until oats are a very fine consistency. Add walnuts and blend until nuts are ground to a chopped consistency.
2. Add rest of ingredients, *except* banana, to blender and "pulse" until mixture is smooth.
3. Pour mixture into a bowl. Add a little water as necessary if mixture thickens too much.
4. Pour onto a preheated, nonstick griddle or pan until golden brown. You do not need oil if you are using a nonstick griddle or pan.
5. Place oatcakes on plates and top with banana. Serve hot.
6. Drizzle with agave nectar or maple syrup as desired. I prefer agave nectar because it is sweeter and requires much less.

BRAIN BOOSTERS
50 best brain foods: oats, walnuts, unsweetened almond milk

Nutrition Per Serving	
275 Calories	6 g Protein
40 g Carbohydrates	8 g Fat
1 g Saturated Fat	0 mg Cholesterol
333 mg Sodium	6 g Fiber

♦　**6 Servings**　♦　**207 Calories**　♦　**5 Brain Boosters**　♦　**Gluten-Free**

Ingredients:

1½ cups rice or coconut yogurt (flavor of your choice)

1 tablespoon ground flax seeds

½ cup Egg Beaters

½ cup almond milk, unsweetened

⅔ cup buckwheat flour or spelt four

2 packets stevia sweetener

1 tablespoon refined coconut oil

2 cups mixed berries and bananas

Optional: 4 tablespoons soy or rice protein powder (or any protein powder of your choice)

This is truly one of the simplest breakfast recipes in the book, and one that your children are sure to love. Although I prefer my daughter to eat some greens for breakfast, this is always good in a pinch, and it ensures good protein intake. It is also a good recipe for company or those who aren't quite on board with your "green" ways yet. This is one of the recipes I like to use to "tease" people into our healthy lifestyle, showing them that eating brain healthy foods doesn't have to be boring.

Preparation:

1. In a small bowl, combine yogurt, protein powder (if desired), and flax seeds. Set aside.
2. In a medium mixing bowl, blend Egg Beaters, almond milk, flour, and stevia. Mix well.
3. Heat oil in a medium skillet over medium heat.
4. Pour ¼ of the batter onto the skillet. Quickly spread the batter across the skillet by lifting and turning until the batter spreads evenly. When the edges of the crepe begin to brown and lift, carefully lift and flip the crepe. Cook until both sides are lightly browned, about 2 minutes.
5. Place each crepe on a plate as they are finished.
6. Spoon yogurt mix into each crepe, top with fresh berries and fold in half.
7. Serve while crepes are warm.

BRAIN BOOSTERS
50 best brain foods: unsweetened yogurt, eggs, unsweetened almond milk, berries, bananas

Nutrition Per Serving	
207 Calories	6 g Protein
35 g Carbohydrates	4 g Fat
2 g Saturated Fat	0 mg Cholesterol
142 mg Sodium	6 g Fiber

♦ **4 Servings** ♦ **252 Calories** ♦ **6 Brain Boosters**

Ingredients:

1 cup almond milk, unsweetened

1 cup water

1 cup rinsed quinoa

1 tablespoon Earth Balance

4 drops vanilla-flavored stevia

1 cup fresh blueberries

1 cup fresh strawberries, sliced

½ teaspoon ground cinnamon

¼ cup raw walnuts, chopped

Preparation:

1. In a medium saucepan over high heat, combine almond milk, water, and quinoa. Bring to a boil. Reduce heat to medium low. Cover and simmer until most of the liquid is absorbed, about 15 minutes.
2. Add Earth Balance and stevia (if desired) and stir well.
3. Remove from heat and let stand for 5 minutes.
4. Stir in blueberries, strawberries, and cinnamon.
5. Top with walnuts and serve warm.

Optional: Drizzle each serving with a little agave nectar. The fruit sweetens this dish enough that even my six-year-old prefers it without the agave nectar. But for those of you with a killer sweet tooth or PMS, a little agave goes a long way.

BRAIN BOOSTERS
50 best brain foods: unsweetened almond milk, water, blueberries, strawberries, walnuts
Brain healthy spices: cinnamon

Nutrition Per Serving

252 Calories	7 g Protein
32 g Carbohydrates	11 g Fat
1 g Saturated Fat	0 mg Cholesterol
76 mg Sodium	5 g Fiber

A LESSON ON LECITHIN: *Be aware that without eggs the cake does not stick together as well as traditional cake. I usually just explain this and no one ever complains. The lecithin helps with this. Lecithin is actually sold as a "health food supplement." Try cutting smaller pieces to counter this minor problem.*

◆ **12 Servings** ◆ **172 Calories** ◆ **3 Brain Boosters** ◆ **Gluten-Free**

Ingredients:

1½ cups oat flour

½ cup brown rice flour

¾ cup agave nectar

1½ teaspoon baking soda

½ teaspoon Real Salt

2 teaspoons cinnamon

1½ cups water

1 teaspoon fresh ground ginger

½ cup safflower oil

¼ teaspoon maple extract

¼ cup apple cider vinegar

½ teaspoon vanilla

¾ cup pecans, finely chopped

Optional: ¼ cup raisins

Optional: 2 teaspoons lecithin granules (to help hold the bars together and make less "crumbly")

This is one of my most popular recipes with guests. I often serve it as a dessert cake. Though we try to limit sugar and starches, this is another "hook" into our healthy lifestyle. I find that people are routinely shocked that food that is gluten-free and has very little sugar can taste this good. It opens their minds to other possibilities.

Preparation:

1. Preheat oven to 350 degrees F.
2. In a large bowl mix oat flour, rice flour, baking soda, salt, cinnamon, and lecithin granules. Set aside.
3. Pour water into a medium bowl. Add one ingredient at a time to the water: ground ginger, agave, oil, maple extract, apple cider vinegar, and vanilla.
4. Pour wet ingredients into large bowl of dry ingredients slowly and beat until mixture is smooth. Stir in raisins, if desired.
5. Pour into 12 x 14 inch oiled cake pan. Sprinkle pecans over the top of mixture.
6. Bake for approximately 45 minutes. Test cake at 40 minutes by inserting a knife into the center and pulling out. If knife comes out "clean," the cake is finished. If knife comes out with cake on it bake for another 5 minutes or so.
7. Cool for a few minutes before cutting or cake will fall apart.
8. Cut into 12 slices and serve warm.

BRAIN BOOSTERS
50 best brain foods: water
Brain healthy spices: cinnamon, ginger

Nutrition Per Serving

172 Calories	3 g Protein
26 g Carbohydrates	7 g Fat
1 g Saturated Fat	0 mg Cholesterol
251 mg Sodium	2 g Fiber

CRANAPPLE WALNUT MUFFINS

♦ **12 Servings** ♦ **216 Calories** ♦ **4 Brain Boosters** ♦ **Gluten-Free**

Ingredients:

1½ cups spelt flour

1½ cups brown rice flour

1¼ cups quick-cooking oats

1 teaspoon ground cinnamon

½ teaspoon nutmeg

1½ teaspoons baking soda

2 packets stevia

12 ounces apple juice concentrate

2 large apples, finely chopped

½ cup walnuts, chopped

½ cup dried cranberries (you can omit cranberries if you wish to decrease the overall sugar content)

Optional: Egg beaters (equivalent of 2 eggs). You can skip this, but muffins will be a bit more dense and dry.

This is another *really* simple recipe. It only takes about 15 minutes of preparation and guests and children really love them. I often make these for my daughter's friends when they come over for "play dates." Since most of them are used to having cookies, candy, and chips at home, I don't want to be the "mean, drill sergeant mom" who only offers carrots and wheat grass. While it isn't sugar free, it is *much* better than what can be found in stores, and because of the healthy ingredients, the children are satisfied and full after eating one.

This should not be your first breakfast choice, but with the added walnuts you will get some healthy fat and protein. They are easy to prepare the night before and "grab-n-go" in the morning. Having a gluten-free cranapple muffin with walnuts certainly beats missing breakfast and being tempted to stop for a sausage-and-egg sandwich at the local drive-thru or an apple fritter at the nearest doughnut shop.

Preparation:

1. Preheat oven to 325 degrees F.
2. In a large mixing bowl, blend spelt flour, rice flour, oats, cinnamon, nutmeg, baking soda, and stevia.
3. Add apple juice concentrate, chopped apple, eggs (if desired), walnuts, and cranberries. Stir just enough to blend.
4. Spoon into nonstick muffin tins.
5. Bake for 25 minutes. Test by touching muffin tops. Tops should not sink when touched, but have some "bounce."

BRAIN BOOSTERS
50 best brain foods: oats, apples, walnuts
Brain healthy spices: cinnamon

Nutrition Per Serving

216 Calories	6 g Protein
37 g Carbohydrates	5 g Fat
0 g Saturated Fat	0 mg Cholesterol
173 mg Sodium	4 g Fiber

CHAPTER 4

Brain Boosting Salads

Salads are a critical component to a brain healthy life. When done right they provide plenty of vegetables, fruits, healthy oils, seeds, nuts, and fiber. Here are some of our favorite recipes.

♦   8 Servings   ♦   201 Calories   ♦   5 Brain Boosters

Ingredients:

3 cups shredded kale or Swiss chard

½ cup shredded green cabbage

½ cup shredded purple cabbage

Optional: Use 1 cup prepackaged coleslaw mix instead of cabbage

¼ cup shredded carrot

½ cup chopped raw cashews

½ cup Veganaise

1 tablespoon apple cider vinegar

½ teaspoon allspice

⅛ teaspoon cinnamon

⅛ teaspoon nutmeg

1 teaspoon fresh oregano, finely chopped (or ½ teaspoon dried)

1 teaspoon fresh thyme (or ½ teaspoon dried)

⅓ teaspoon curry powder

¼ teaspoon Real Salt

¼ teaspoon pepper

¼ cup raw sunflower seeds

½ cup dried cranberries

Preparation:

1. Combine kale, cabbage, carrot, and nuts.
2. In a small mixing bowl, combine Veganaise, vinegar, stevia (if desired), and spices. Whisk until mixture is blended well.
3. Toss with salad mix.
4. Allow salad to refrigerate for 30 minutes prior to serving if possible so flavors can "marry." This salad actually tastes better the following day after the flavors marry and the kale has a chance to absorb some of the dressing.
5. Top with sunflower seeds and dried cranberries.

Optional: Try combining the ingredients for the dressing — listed in Step 2 — in a blender or food processor with ¼ cup sesame oil and ½ cup raw peanuts or almonds. I'm not a big fan of peanuts, but they give great flavor to the dressing. Purée and pour over salad blend. Toss well.

BRAIN BOOSTERS
50 best brain foods: carrots
Brain healthy spices: cinnamon, oregano, thyme, curry

Nutrition Per Serving

201 Calories	3 g Protein
14 g Carbohydrates	14 g Fat
2 g Saturated Fat	0 mg Cholesterol
187 mg Sodium	3 g Fiber

♦ **10 Servings** ♦ **188 Calories** ♦ **8 Brain Boosters**

Ingredients:

1 cup quinoa

1 red onion, thinly sliced

1 tablespoon refined coconut oil

1½-2 teaspoons cumin

2 cups water

1 15-ounce can black beans, drained

2 cups cherry tomatoes, halved

¼ cup fresh basil, chopped

2 tablespoons pine nuts

2 avocados, diced

1 red bell pepper, finely chopped

⅓ cup cilantro, finely chopped

1 bunch green onion, finely chopped

2 celery stalks, finely chopped

4 tablespoons fresh lime juice

3 tablespoons flax seed oil or extra virgin olive oil

Real Salt to taste

Preparation:

1. Bring the quinoa and water to boil, then reduce to a simmer and cook until the water is absorbed, approximately 10 minutes. When quinoa is finished strain and rinse well under cold water.

2. Meanwhile, in a medium skillet heat coconut oil over medium heat and sauté red onions until transparent, approximately 3-5 minutes. Let cool.

3. In a large mixing bowl, mix all ingredients together. Toss well.

Bon appétit!

BRAIN BOOSTERS

50 best brain foods: water, black beans, tomatoes, avocados, red bell pepper, limes, olive oil
Brain healthy spices: basil

Nutrition Per Serving

188 Calories	6 g Protein
25 g Carbohydrates	7 g Fat
1 g Saturated Fat	0 mg Cholesterol
90 mg Sodium	7 g Fiber

♦ **4 Servings** ♦ **172 Calories** ♦ **6 Brain Boosters**

Ingredients:

4 small Persian cucumbers or 1 large cucumber, cut into thin slices
1 red bell pepper, diced
½ cup grape tomatoes, halved
½ cup edamame (soybeans), shelled and cooked
1 carrot, grated

Dressing Ingredients:

2 teaspoons tahini
1 garlic clove or shallot, quartered
2 tablespoons sesame oil or pea-nut oil
2 teaspoons rice wine vinegar (with no sugar added)
2 tablespoons low-sodium soy sauce *or* 2 teaspoons Bragg Liquid AminoS
2 teaspoons fresh ginger root, diced or grated
½ teaspoon Real Salt
¼ teaspoon black pepper
1 tablespoon black sesame seeds

Preparation:

1. For dressing: In a blender, put tahini, garlic (or shallot), vinegar, soy sauce, ginger, salt, and pepper. Blend briefly.
2. While blender is running, add oil in a slow stream. Set dressing aside.
3. In a salad bowl, toss together cucumbers, red pepper, tomatoes, edamame, and carrot.
4. Either dish salad mix into bowls and drizzle a small amount of dressing onto each salad or toss dressing into the entire salad mix before dishing.
5. Sprinkle with sesame seeds before serving.

BRAIN BOOSTERS
50 best brain foods: red bell pepper, tomatoes, soybeans, carrots
Brain healthy spices: garlic, ginger

Nutrition Per Serving

172 Calories	4 g Protein
14 g Carbohydrates	11 g Fat
1 g Saturated Fat	0 mg Cholesterol
595 mg Sodium	3 g Fiber

◆ **8 Servings** ◆ **139 Calories** ◆ **4 Brain Boosters**

Ingredients:

¾ cup barley

¼ cup extra virgin olive oil

1½ teaspoons fresh lemon juice

½ teaspoon fine sea salt

¼ teaspoon pepper

1 tomato, finely diced

1 cucumber, peeled and finely diced

¼ red onion, finely diced

½ cup red bell pepper, finely diced

⅓ cup parsley, roughly chopped

⅓ cup fresh mint, roughly chopped

This is a refreshing alternative to traditional tabouleh, which is typically made with bulghur wheat. Additionally, this recipe has less parsley (although parsley is actually OUTSTANDING for you, it can be somewhat overwhelming and an acquired taste) and some additional other vegetables. This salad is very substantial and filling, and usually a hit with most guests. It doesn't get any healthier. Even my six-year-old loves this one!

Preparation:

1. Prepare barley 45 minutes in advance according to directions. Barley will make double amount when cooked.
2. In a small mixing bowl, combine olive oil, lemon juice, salt, and pepper. Set aside.
3. When barley has cooled, place in a large mixing bowl. Add tomato, cucumber, onion, bell pepper, parsley, and mint.
4. Add in oil and lemon juice dressing mixture. Toss gently. Add more lemon juice and salt if necessary.
5. Refrigerate for 10 minutes or so. This salad should be served cool.

Optional: Sometimes I prefer a higher vegetable-to-barley ratio. You can always add a little cucumber and bell pepper if desired.

BRAIN BOOSTERS
50 best brain foods: olive oil, lemons, red bell pepper, tomatoes

Nutrition Per Serving

139 Calories	3 g Protein
17 g Carbohydrates	4 g Fat
1 g Saturated Fat	0 mg Cholesterol
7 mg Sodium	4 g Fiber

SALADS

♦ **8 Servings** ♦ **90 Calories** ♦ **8 Brain Boosters**

Ingredients:

1 peach, sliced

1 cup red or green grapes (or mixed)

½ cup fresh blueberries

½ cup fresh strawberries, sliced

1 banana, sliced

1 tangerine, peeled and pieced

½ cup fresh raspberries for salad

1 cup fresh raspberries for dressing

1 cup coconut milk yogurt, vanilla or plain (dairy free)

¼ cup fresh mint, coarsely chopped

Optional: 1 tablespoon agave nectar or honey

Optional: 1 tablespoon fresh lime juice

This recipe is great for breakfast as well as dessert. It is always a hit. The mint is a refreshing twist.

Preparation:

1. In a large salad bowl, mix all fresh fruit together. Be careful not to crush berries and bananas.
2. In a blender, mix 1 cup raspberries, yogurt, and fresh mint as well as agave nectar and lime juice (if desired). Dressing may be plenty sweet with only the yogurt for flavor.
3. Slowly pour dressing over fruit salad until desired amount is achieved. Do not use too much dressing or it will overwhelm the taste of the fruit. It is better to start with a small amount and add more if necessary.
4. Serve cold in martini glasses or ice cream dishes.

BRAIN BOOSTERS

50 best brain foods: peaches, strawberries, blueberries, bananas, tangerines (same as oranges), raspberries, unsweetened yogurt, limes

Nutrition Per Serving

90 Calories	1 g Protein
20 g Carbohydrates	2 g Fat
1 g Saturated Fat	0 mg Cholesterol
4 mg Sodium	4 g Fiber

BREAKFAST ON THE GO: *To simplify this recipe for breakfast on the go, simply add coconut milk yogurt and flax seeds to the fruit salad and mix. This adds a little protein and some live cultures to your morning start.*

SALADS

♦ **4 Servings** ♦ **188 Calories** ♦ **5 Brain Boosters**

Ingredients:

1 cup fresh green beans, cut in 1 inch pieces
4 fresh ripe tangerines, peeled and pieced
½ cup sweet red onion, thinly sliced
½ cup edamame beans (soybeans), removed from skins
2 tablespoons sunflower seeds

Tahini Dressing Ingredients:

2 teaspoons tahini
1 garlic clove or shallot, quartered
2 tablespoons sesame oil
2 teaspoons rice wine vinegar (with no sugar added)
2 tablespoons low-sodium soy sauce *or* 2 teaspoons Bragg Liquid Aminos
2 teaspoons fresh ginger root, diced or grated
½ teaspoon Real Salt
¼ teaspoon black pepper

Dressing Preparation:

1. In a blender, put tahini, garlic (or shallot), vinegar, soy sauce, ginger, salt, and pepper. Blend briefly.
2. While blender is running add oil in a slow stream. Set dressing aside.

Preparation:

1. Place green beans in boiling water for about 3 or 4 minutes. Make sure they remain crisp. Remove and immediately rinse with cool water.
2. Take tangerine slices and gently try to remove white pulpy portions, be sure to remove visible seeds. Do this over the salad mixing bowl to catch tangerine juice.
3. In the salad bowl, mix green beans, onion, edamame, and tangerine.
4. Drizzle with dressing of choice and top with sunflower seeds.

BRAIN BOOSTERS
50 best brain foods: soybeans, tangerines (same as oranges), olive oil
Brain healthy spices: garlic, ginger

Nutrition Per Serving with Dressing	
188 Calories	5 g Protein
19 g Carbohydrates	11 g Fat
2 g Saturated Fat	0 mg Cholesterol
862 mg Sodium	7 g Fiber

Nutrition Per Serving, Dressing Alone	
82 Calories	1 g Protein
2 g Carbohydrates	8 g Fat
1 g Saturated Fat	0 mg Cholesterol
572 mg Sodium	0 g Fiber

♦ **6 Servings** ♦ **66 Calories** ♦ **5 Brain Boosters**

Ingredients:

6 ounces baby spinach
1 avocado, peeled and cut into
    large chunks
1 garlic clove
1 tablespoon fresh lemon juice
3 tablespoons cilantro
6 tablespoons soy cream
20 cherry tomatoes, halved
¼ sweet red onion, thinly sliced
Real Salt to taste

Preparation:

1. Add avocado, garlic, lemon juice, cilantro, and soy cream in blender. Blend until smooth and creamy.
2. Toss dressing mixture with spinach in a large bowl with onions.
3. Add tomatoes.
4. Add Real Salt to taste.

BRAIN BOOSTERS

50 best brain foods: spinach, avocado, lemons, tomatoes
Brain healthy spices: garlic

Nutrition Per Serving	
66 Calories	2 g Protein
6 g Carbohydrates	5 g Fat
1 g Saturated Fat	0 mg Cholesterol
28 mg Sodium	3 g Fiber

♦ **6 Servings** ♦ **130 Calories** ♦ **4 Brain Boosters**

Ingredients:

1 bunch mint, stems removed
1 bunch parsley, stems removed
2 cucumbers, minced
1 red bell pepper, finely
chopped
6 scallions, minced
4 tomatoes, seeded and finely
chopped
½ cup fresh lemon juice
¼ cup olive oil
½ teaspoon Real Salt
½ teaspoon paprika

Preparation:

1. Finely mince mint and parsley by hand or in food processor if preferred.
2. In large mixing bowl, blend herbs with cucumber, bell pepper, scallions, and tomatoes.
3. Add lemon juice, olive oil, and spices.
4. Toss and serve.

BRAIN BOOSTERS
50 best brain foods: red bell pepper, tomatoes, lemons, olive oil

Nutrition Per Serving

130 Calories   2 g Protein
12 g Carbohydrates   9 g Fat
2 g Saturated Fat   0 mg Cholesterol
205 mg Sodium   3 g Fiber

CHAPTER 5
Soups to Heal the Hardware of Your Soul

A number of years ago my husband wrote a book called *Healing The Hardware of the Soul*. He argued that the brain is the hardware of the soul and when it works right we are more thoughtful, more loving, and more effective in everything we do. This chapter is one of his favorite parts of this cookbook. He says these recipes soothe his soul. The recipes are filled with brain healthy nutrients to help you think better and live longer. The first recipe is his favorite. He also loves the salmon curry chowder. Not only because it tastes great, but because it can also make you smarter. Enjoy!

♦ **8 Servings** ♦ **81 Calories** ♦ **6 Brain Boosters**

Ingredients:

½ cup onion, diced

⅓ cup celery, diced

3 tablespoons leeks, diced

2 garlic cloves, minced

6-7 cups vegetable stock

1½ pounds sweet potatoes,
 peeled and diced

1 cinnamon stick

¼ teaspoon nutmeg

1 teaspoon Real Salt

1 teaspoon white pepper

½ cup almond milk

2 tablespoons fresh sage, finely chopped

¼ cup sunflower seeds (optional)

⅛ cup cranberries

Cinnamon, sprinkled for garnish

Preparation:

1. Heat ¼ cup of vegetable broth in large soup pot over medium heat. Sauté onions, celery, and leeks for 2 minutes. Then add garlic and sauté for another minute.
2. Add 4 cups of remaining vegetable broth, sweet potatoes, cinnamon stick, and nutmeg. Bring to a boil then reduce heat to medium-low and simmer until potatoes are tender, about 10 minutes.
3. Remove cinnamon stick.
4. Use immersion blender or pour contents into a blender in batches. Blend until smooth.
5. Pour soup back into pot (if using a blender). Add almond milk. Then slowly add remaining broth according to preferred consistency.
6. Add salt and pepper.
7. Dish soup into bowls. Sprinkle sunflower seeds, sage, and cranberries in each bowl and serve.

BRAIN BOOSTERS
50 best brain foods: sweet potatoes, almond milk, cranberries
Brain healthy spices: garlic, cinnamon, sage

Nutrition Per Serving

81 Calories	2 g Protein
17 g Carbohydrates	0 g Fat
0 g Saturated Fat	0 mg Cholesterol
4 mg Sodium	2g Fiber

KAMILA'S AMAZING ASPARAGUS SOUP

♦ **6 Servings** ♦ **80 Calories** ♦ **1 Brain Boosters**

SOUPS

Ingredients:

1 pound asparagus (thickness irrelevant)

1-2 tablespoons refined coconut oil

½ cup large white onion, finely chopped

1 leek, chopped (do not use green leafy portion)

¼ cup celery, chopped

1 tablespoon fresh tarragon

3 cups vegetable stock

1 tablespoon flour

Real Salt and pepper to taste

2 tablespoons soy creamer (optional)

Preparation:

1. Cut off asparagus tips and reserve. Discard tough ends. Chop remaining stems.
2. In medium soup pot heat refined coconut oil. Sauté onions, leeks, celery, and asparagus stems over medium heat until onions are translucent, about 5 minutes.
3. Add flour and stir until well blended. Stir well while cooking, about 1 minute more.
4. Transfer vegetables and flour mixture to a blender. Add about 1 cup of vegetable broth (enough to help mixture blend easily). Blend well and transfer back to pot.
5. Add remaining vegetable stock to pot gradually, stirring out any lumps. Bring soup mixture to a boil then reduce heat and simmer until the soup is smooth and thickened, about 30-40 minutes. Stir frequently.
6. Add soy creamer if desired. Add salt and pepper as desired for tasted.
7. Add asparagus tips to soup and simmer 5-10 minutes.
8. Add tarragon for flavor.
9. Serve warm.

Optional: Sprinkle with whole grain croutons or make your own by toasting whole grain bread until hard.

BRAIN BOOSTERS
50 best brain foods: asparagus

Nutrition Per Serving

80 Calories	3 g Protein
10 g Carbohydrates	4 g Fat
1 g Saturated Fat	0 mg Cholesterol
520 mg Sodium	2 g Fiber

♦ **6 Servings** ♦ **111 Calories** ♦ **9 Brain Boosters**

Ingredients:

4 small red potatoes, quartered
1 tablespoon refined coconut oil
1 small onion, finely chopped
2 cloves garlic, minced
8 cups organic vegetable broth
Water, as needed
1 bunch celery, cut into 1-inch pieces
½ head cauliflower, cut into small florets
½ head broccoli, cut into small florets
¼ cup parsley, finely chopped
1 cup carrots, diced
1 cup fresh green beans, cut into 1-inch pieces
½ red bell pepper, chopped
1 tomato, chopped
1 cup baby spinach leaves
½-inch fresh ginger, sliced
1 tablespoon fresh basil, finely chopped
1 teaspoon Real Salt
½ teaspoon pepper
½ teaspoon cayenne pepper

Preparation:

1. Cook quartered potatoes in boiling water for about 20 minutes (until tender).
2. In separate soup pot, over low heat, sauté onion in coconut oil for about 3 minutes.
3. Add garlic and sauté for additional 2 minutes.
4. Add vegetable broth, celery, cauliflower, broccoli, parsley, carrots, red bell pepper, and green beans. Heat until veggies are warm and slightly tender, but still crisp, about 3-5 minutes.
5. Add tomatoes, spinach leaves, ginger, basil, salt, pepper, and cayenne.
6. Reduce heat to low and simmer for 10 minutes to allow flavors to "marry."

Optional: If you are not an onion and garlic lover, skipping the onion and garlic will save you the step of sautéing.

BRAIN BOOSTERS
50 best brain foods: water, broccoli, carrots, red bell pepper, tomatoes, spinach
Brain healthy spices: garlic, ginger, basil

CAPTAIN CRUNCH: *I prefer vegetables to be crunchy because they are more nutritious that way. If you prefer your vegetables to be very tender you may need to allow more time for simmering.*

Nutrition Per Serving

111 Calories	4 g Protein
19 g Carbohydrates	3 g Fat
2 g Saturated Fat	0 mg Cholesterol
1716 mg Sodium	5 g Fiber

SOUPS

SAVORY SPINACH BARLEY SOUP

♦ **6 Servings** ♦ **110 Calories** ♦ **4 Brain Boosters**

Ingredients:

¼ cup vegetable broth or 2 table spoons refined coconut oil
1 yellow onion, diced
1 tablespoon garlic, minced
6 cups vegetable broth
1½ cups barley, cooked
1 pound baby spinach, stems removed
3 large tomatoes, peeled, deseeded, and chopped
1 tablespoon fresh basil, minced
1 teaspoon Real Salt
½ teaspoon black pepper

Advance Preparation:

1. Peel and deseed the tomatoes. Drop room-temperature tomatoes into boiling water. Leave in water for about 30 seconds. Do not leave tomatoes in water too long. Remove from boiling water and rinse tomatoes in cold water. Use a sharp knife to pierce the skins. Skins should come off easily. Chop tomatoes and set aside.
2. Cook barley as directed on package.

Preparation:

1. In a 6-quart pot, use broth or coconut oil over medium heat and sauté onions and garlic in oil for about 3 minutes or until onions look translucent.
2. Add remaining vegetable stock and bring to a boil. Reduce heat to medium low.
3. Add barley to vegetable stock and simmer for 10 minutes.
4. Stir in tomatoes and spinach and simmer another 5 minutes.
5. Add basil, salt, and pepper.
6. Serve in soup bowls.

Optional: Garnish with vegan cheese or toasted whole wheat croutons.

BRAIN BOOSTERS
50 best brain foods: spinach, tomatoes
Brain healthy spices: garlic, basil

Nutrition Per Serving	
110 Calories	4g Protein
23 g Carbohydrates	1 g Fat
0 g Saturated Fat	0 mg Cholesterol
1436 mg Sodium	5 g Fiber

CREATIVE CREAMY CAULIFLOWER SOUP

◆ **6 Servings** ◆ **145 Calories** ◆ **5 Brain Boosters**

Ingredients:

2 tablespoons coconut oil
2 yellow squash, sliced thinly
2 zucchini, sliced thinly
1 small onion, diced
1 celery stalk, cut into 1-inch pieces
2 garlic cloves, minced
1 teaspoon fresh rosemary, chopped
1 head of cauliflower, chopped
½ cup ground almonds (this can be done in the food processor or blender)
4-6 cups vegetable broth
2 cups almond milk, unsweetened
½ teaspoon allspice
1 teaspoon fresh sage, chopped
Real Salt and pepper
Dash of nutmeg

Preparation:

1. Preheat oven to broil. Place zucchini and squash on cookie sheet and brush lightly with 1 tablespoon refined coconut oil. Broil until lightly browned, about 10 minutes. Set aside.
2. In a large soup pot, heat 1 tablespoon of refined coconut oil. Sauté onions and celery until onions are translucent, about 2-3 minutes.
3. Add garlic and rosemary, sauté for additional minute.
4. Add in cauliflower, almonds, and 4 cups of vegetable stock. Bring to a boil then reduce heat to a simmer for about 15 minutes.
5. Use either a hand-held blender, or place soup mix in a traditional blender and blend until mixture is smooth. Put mixture back into pot.
6. Put grilled zucchini and squash into a food processor and pulse chop until finely minced. Add to the soup mix.
7. Add almond milk and allspice. Stir until warmed through.
8. At this time you may choose to add more vegetable broth if desired, depending on how thick you prefer your soup to be.
9. Stir in sage, salt, and pepper.
10. Serve in soup bowls and sprinkle with nutmeg.

BRAIN BOOSTERS
50 best brain foods: almonds, almond milk
Brain healthy spices: garlic, rosemary, sage

Nutrition Per Serving	
145 Calories	5 g Protein
17 g Carbohydrates	8 g Fat
4 g Saturated Fat	0 mg Cholesterol
980 mg Sodium	6 g Fiber

♦ **6 Servings** ♦ **92 Calories** ♦ **6 Brain Boosters**

Ingredients:

2 tablespoons refined coconut oil or vegetable broth

⅔ cup carrot, diced

½ cup celery, diced

½ onion, diced

1 garlic clove, minced

4 cups butternut squash, peeled and cubed

1 teaspoon fresh thyme

1 tablespoon of ginger, grated

4 cups vegetable broth

½ cup soy creamer

Real Salt and white pepper to taste

Preparation:

1. Heat oil or vegetable broth in a large soup pot over medium high heat. Add carrot, celery, and onion and cook until vegetables begin to soften, about 3 minutes.
2. Add garlic and cook until fragrant, about 1 minute.
3. Add butternut squash and thyme. Stir.
4. Add ginger and stir for about a minute.
5. Add broth and bring to a boil. Simmer for 15 minutes.
6. Use an immersion blender or pour soup in batches into a food processor or blender.
7. Pour soup back into soup pot that has been rinsed.
8. Stir in soy creamer.
9. Add salt and white pepper.
10. Stir over medium heat until warmed through.
11. Ladle into soup tureen and garnish with thyme.
12. Serve warm

BRAIN BOOSTERS
50 best brain foods: carrots, apples
Brain healthy spices: garlic, thyme, sage, cinnamon

Nutrition Per Serving	
92 Calories	2 g Protein
23 g Carbohydrates	0 g Fat
0 g Saturated Fat	0 mg Cholesterol
652 mg Sodium	6 g Fiber

BRAIN FOOD SALMON CURRY CHOWDER

◆ **6 Servings** ◆ **403 Calories** ◆ **6 Brain Boosters**

Ingredients:

1 pound fresh wild salmon
Vegetarian option: Replace salmon with firm tofu
2-3 teaspoons refined coconut oil
1 teaspoon Real Salt
½ teaspoon pepper
4 small new potatoes, diced (organic)
1 yellow onion, diced
8 celery stalks, chopped
3 carrots, chopped
1 14-ounce can coconut milk
2 cups almond milk, unsweetened
½ teaspoon Thai green curry paste
½ teaspoon vanilla
1 cup fresh peas
1 cup fresh spinach

This dish is traditionally made with salmon. However, for vegetarians, tofu substitutes for fish nicely.

Preparation:

1. Sprinkle fish with salt and pepper.
2. Heat coconut oil in pan over medium heat and fry fish until cooked through. Do not overcook. Make sure fish remains moist. Cut into bite-size chunks and set aside.
3. Heat a small amount of refined coconut oil or vegetable broth in pan over medium heat. Sauté potatoes, onion, celery, and carrots briefly, but do not overcook, about 5 minutes. Add coconut milk, almond milk, green curry paste, and vanilla. Mix well.
4. Add salmon to base and stir.
5. Take ⅓ of entire soup mixture and transfer to blender to purée. Transfer puréed mixture back to soup pot and mix well. You may skip this step to save time or if you prefer a thinner soup base. However, this step makes the soup more like "chowder."
6. Add peas and spinach shortly before serving.
7. Serve in soup tureens.

BRAIN BOOSTERS
50 best brain foods: wild salmon (or tofu), carrots, unsweetened almond milk, peas, spinach
Brain healthy spices: curry

Nutrition Per Serving

403 Calories	24 g Protein
21 g Carbohydrates	26 g Fat
17 g Saturated Fat	54 mg Cholesterol
576 mg Sodium	5 g Fiber

LIFE-ENHANCING LENTIL SOUP

♦ **8 Servings** ♦ **212 Calories** ♦ **9 Brain Boosters**

Ingredients:

¼ cup vegetable broth for sautéing vegetables, or 1 table spoon refined coconut oil
4 celery stalks, cut into ½-inch pieces
1 carrot, cut into ½-inch pieces
1 red bell pepper, chopped
2 onions, chopped
2 garlic cloves, minced
6 cups water
6 cups vegetable broth
2 cups red lentils
¼ cup brown rice
1 tablespoon fresh marjoram, finely chopped (optional)
1 tablespoon fresh sage, finely chopped (optional)
2 teaspoons garlic salt (or to taste)
½ teaspoon curry powder
½ teaspoon ground cumin
1 tablespoon lemon pepper
1 teaspoon pepper
1 tablespoon fresh lemon juice

Preparation:

1. In a large soup pot, heat vegetable broth (preferably) or refined coconut oil. Sauté celery, carrot, red bell peppers, onion, and garlic for about 5 minutes.
2. Add water and vegetable broth to pot. Stir in lentils and rice. Cover and bring to a boil. Reduce heat and simmer, stirring occasionally for about 25 minutes.
3. Stir in herbs, garlic salt, curry, cumin, lemon pepper, and pepper. Simmer uncovered for about 20 minutes, or until lentils fall apart and mixture thickens.
4. Stir in lemon juice.
5. Ladle into soup bowls and garnish with cilantro or parsley as desired.

BRAIN BOOSTERS
50 best brain foods: carrots, red bell peppers, water, lentils, lemons
Brain healthy spices: garlic, marjoram, sage, curry

Nutrition Per Serving

212 Calories	14g Protein
37 g Carbohydrates	1 g Fat
0 g Saturated Fat	0 mg Cholesterol
802 mg Sodium	9g Fiber

SOUPS

CHAPTER 6
Brain Power Lunches

If you want to stop feeling sluggish in the afternoon, having a nutritious lunch is critical. Here are some great recipes to help you feel happy and energetic.

SCRUMPTIOUS SOUTHWESTERN TACOS

◆   **4 Servings**   ◆   **218 Calories**   ◆   **4 Brain Boosters**

LUNCH

Ingredients:

1 head romaine lettuce, leaves whole

2 teaspoons refined coconut oil

2 cloves garlic, minced

1 tablespoon shallot, minced

2 Boca burgers (or other vegetarian-style burger patties)

½ cup roasted or raw red bell pepper, diced (I prefer raw)

⅓ cup jicama, diced

½ cup tomatillo, diced

½ cup, diced vine-ripened tomatoes (see "Tomato Tips")

1 tablespoon cilantro, chopped

1 ripe avocado, peeled and diced

¼ teaspoon Real Salt

¼ cup sunflower seeds

1 cup fresh salsa (fresh salsa can be made or bought fresh at your local health food store)

Optional: ½ teaspoon jalapeno, minced (with seeds makes salad spicier; removing seeds makes it milder)

Optional: ½ package organic taco seasoning

Preparation:

1. In advance, use whole, large romaine leaves to line a large platter. Set aside.
2. Heat oil in large skillet over medium heat. Add garlic, shallots, and jalapeno if desired. Sautee for about 1 minute.
3. Add Boca burgers and break apart into crumbles with spatula or spoon. Stir and sauté until burgers are lightly browned, about 2 minutes. Sprinkle mixture with taco seasoning if desired, and add a tablespoon or two of water if necessary, but not too much water. You may not need the taco seasoning depending on the flavor of Boca burger you choose. Many of them are already flavored.
4. Add red bell peppers, jicama, tomatillo, and tomatoes. Stir until lightly warmed.
5. Take off heat. Stir in cilantro and salt.
6. Dish salad mix into the lettuce shells. Top with avocado and sprinkle with sunflower seeds.
7. Use fresh salsa as a dressing.

BRAIN BOOSTERS
50 best brain foods: red bell pepper, tomatoes, avocado
Brain healthy spices: garlic

Nutrition Per Serving

218 Calories	11 g Protein
18 g Carbohydrates	14 g Fat
3 g Saturated Fat	0 mg Cholesterol
573 mg Sodium	9 g Fiber

TOMATO TIPS: *Instead of diced vine-ripened tomatoes, you may wish to use peeled and seeded tomatoes because they look better without the skins. This is known as tomato concasse. To do this put ripe tomatoes in boiling water for 30-60 seconds. Remove and run under cold water. Peel, slice, and remove seeds. I prefer using the whole tomato to preserve the nutritional integrity.*

GRILLED VEGGIE SANDWICH

♦ **4 Servings** ♦ **604 Calories** ♦ **5 Brain Boosters**

LUNCH

Ingredients:

8 garlic cloves (optional)
1 tablespoon thyme, chopped
2 tablespoons basil, chopped
½ teaspoon Real Salt
½ teaspoon pepper
1½ teaspoons red wine vinegar
½ cup refined coconut oil,
warm for a few seconds to melt
1 eggplant, cut lengthwise into
thin slices
1 zucchini, cut lengthwise into
thin slices
2 red bell peppers, cut into
wedges
8 green onions
4 whole grain, sprouted grain,
or gluten-free rolls
4 leaves of romaine lettuce
1 tomato, sliced

Dressing Ingredients:

2 tablespoons balsamic vinegar
3 tablespoons olive oil

Preparation:

1. Preheat oven to 350 degrees F. Place garlic in small glass Pyrex cup and cover with foil. Bake for about 30-35 minutes, until tender. Cool and mash.

2. Preheat grill to medium.

3. In a large bowl, combine the thyme and basil, the salt, black pepper, vinegar, and oil. Add the eggplant, zucchini, bell peppers, and onion and stir to coat. Grill the vegetables in batches, turning once, until lightly browned and tender, 10 to 15 minutes per batch.

4. Whisk together balsamic vinegar and 3 tablespoons of olive oil in small bowl. This may be one of the few times you end up using olive oil as a marinade and to baste the vegetables. I still use coconut oil, but it is solid unless you heat it, so you must grill the veggies right away.

5. Spread the inside of each roll with 1 tablespoon of the mashed garlic. Place the grilled vegetables, lettuce, and tomatoes in the rolls. Drizzle with vinegar and oil mix (be sure to whisk again and mix well before drizzling).

6. Most of the marinade should be discarded after coating the vegetables and marinating. A thin coat is sufficient. Any more marinade than the amount required for grilling and flavor is excess fat and calories.

BRAIN BOOSTERS
50 best brain foods: red bell pepper, tomatoes
Brain healthy spices: garlic, thyme, basil

Nutrition Per Serving with Dressing	
604 Calories	11 g Protein
55 g Carbohydrates	41 g Fat
25 g Saturated Fat	0 mg Cholesterol
974 mg Sodium	13 g Fiber

Nutrition Per Serving, Dressing Alone	
95 Calories	0 g Protein
2 g Carbohydrates	10 g Fat
1 g Saturated Fat	0 mg Cholesterol
0 mg Sodium	0 g Fiber

◆ **6 Servings** ◆ **249 Calories** ◆ **4 Brain Boosters**

Ingredients:

12 rice paper wrappers
1 cup warm water
6 ounces brown rice noodles
¾ cup carrots, julienned
½ cup almonds, slivered
¼ cup romaine lettuce, finely
shredded
¾ cup bean sprouts
2 tablespoons cilantro
3 tablespoons fresh lemon juice
Real Salt to taste
*Optional: ½ teaspoon stevia or 1
teaspoon agave nectar*
*Optional: 6-8 ounces cooked
shrimp or crab for non-vegetarians*

Dipping Sauce Ingredients:

1 cup low-sodium soy sauce or
tamari
¾ cups fresh lemon juice
¼ cup rice wine vinegar
1 tablespoon minced garlic
Optional: 1 teaspoon chili sauce
*Optional: 1 packet stevia or 1
tablespoon agave nectar*

Preparation:

1. Cook the rice noodles in boiling water, according to the directions on package. When finished cooking, rinse immediately in cold water, drain, and set aside.
2. If using shrimp, slice cooked shrimp lengthwise (finely chop if desired) and set aside.
3. Sprinkle carrots with salt to tenderize them. Set aside for 10 minutes. Rinse in cold water and drain well.
4. To shred lettuce, keep the lettuce leaves stacked, then roll them together and slice the roll in thin sections. When you are finished, you will have long, uniform slivers of lettuce ready for the rolls.
5. Combine noodles, almonds, carrots, shredded lettuce, bean sprouts, cilantro, and lemon juice in a mixing bowl.
6. Combine stevia or agave with warm water in a large bowl. Moisten rice paper in warm water. Place on clean cloth.
7. Put ¼ cup of vegetable filling in center of rice wrapper. Place shrimp if desired on top of vegetable mixture.
8. Fold each end of wrapper and roll to completely encase the contents of wrapper.
9. Serve with fresh ponzu sauce.

Dipping Sauce Preparation:

In a small bowl, whisk together all ingredients until thoroughly blended. Refrigerate until ready to serve.

BRAIN BOOSTERS
50 best brain foods: water, carrots, almonds
Brain healthy spices: garlic

Nutrition Per Serving with Dipping Sauce	
249 Calories	8 g Protein
44 g Carbohydrates	5 g Fat
1 g Saturated Fat	0 mg Cholesterol
1430 mg Sodium	2 g Fiber

Nutrition Per Serving, Dipping Sauce Only	
34 Calories	2 g Protein
7 g Carbohydrates	0 g Fat
0 g Saturated Fat	0 mg Cholesterol
1417 mg Sodium	1 g Fiber

◆ **6 Servings** ◆ **212 Calories** ◆ **6 Brain Boosters**

Ingredients:

16 ounces whole wheat or gluten-free pasta
¼ cup vegetable broth or 3 tablespoons refined coconut oil (for sautéing)
1 small onion, chopped
2 garlic cloves, minced
1 cup asparagus tips
1 cup small broccoli, cut into small florets
1 cup small cauliflower, cut into small florets
1 small zucchini, chopped
½ cup red bell pepper, chopped
1 cup soy cream
2 tablespoons fresh basil, chopped
1 tablespoon fresh oregano, chopped
15 cherry tomatoes, halved
Real Salt and pepper to taste
1 cup vegetable broth
2 teaspoons cornstarch dissolved in water

Preparation:

1. Bring water to a boil in a large pot. Add pasta to boiling water and cook according to instructions while preparing primavera sauce.
2. Heat broth or oil in a large skillet over medium heat. I prefer using broth to sauté vegetables when possible. Sauté onion for a couple minutes, then add garlic and sauté for another minute.
3. Mix in asparagus, broccoli, cauliflower, zucchini, and bell pepper and sauté for 2 minutes. Add remaining vegetable broth, cream, basil, oregano, tomatoes, salt, and pepper.
4. Add cornstarch (previously dissolved in water). Turn up the heat and bring to a boil for 3 minutes. Turn down to a simmer.
5. Drain pasta and toss with primavera sauce.

Suggestion: serve with Pomegranate Walnut Salad.

BRAIN BOOSTERS
50 best brain foods: asparagus, broccoli, red bell pepper, tomatoes
Brain healthy spices: basil, oregano

Nutrition Per Serving

212 Calories	5 g Protein
26 g Carbohydrates	12 g Fat
7 g Saturated Fat	0 mg Cholesterol
206 mg Sodium	4 g Fiber

WARM SPINACH ASPARAGUS SALAD WITH QUINOA

♦ **6 Servings** ♦ **210 Calories** ♦ **4 Brain Boosters**

Ingredients:

3-4 tablespoons vegetable broth for sautéing, or 2 teaspoons refined coconut oil

¼ cup onion, finely diced

4 garlic cloves, diced

1 tablespoon refined coconut oil to coat quinoa

1 cup quinoa, rinsed

2 cups vegetable broth or water

1 bunch asparagus tips

2 handfuls spinach, chopped

1 tablespoon fresh sage (optional)

2 tablespoons chives

¼ cup pine nuts, raw

Real Salt and pepper to taste

Optional: 1 tablespoon olive oil

Optional: 1 tablespoon Bragg Liquid Aminos

This is a great meal option for breakfast or lunch. I usually double the portion so I have leftovers for the next morning. It is a great "breakfast on the run" if you're really busy.

Preparation:

1. Heat 3-4 tablespoons of vegetable broth or 2 tablespoons oil in large pot over medium heat. Sauté onions for 1 minute in broth.
2. Add garlic and sauté for additional minute.
3. Add 1 tablespoon of oil to pot. Add quinoa and stir well to coat lightly with oil.
4. Turn heat up to medium-high and stir quinoa constantly for about 10 minutes or until quinoa is lightly toasted.
5. Add broth and turn heat to high. Bring to a boil. Reduce heat to medium-low and simmer for 15 minutes or until liquid is absorbed.
6. Add asparagus tips to quinoa during last 2 minutes of cooking. This will give you crunchy, healthy asparagus and ensure that they are not overcooked. It also eliminates the step of having to sauté or steam them separately (but if you prefer softer veggies you may cook them separately and add them).
7. Add the spinach to the quinoa while the quinoa is still warm and mix it in. It will wilt the spinach without overcooking it, thus retaining most of the nutritional value. Add sage and chives.
8. *Optional: You may want to toss salad with 1 tablespoon of refined coconut oil or olive oil to fluff the salad and give it a nice texture.*
9. Add pine nuts and stir well. Add salt and pepper to taste.
10. Add Bragg Liquid Aminos, if desired and serve warm. .

Nutrition Per Serving	
210 Calories	8 g Protein
24 g Carbohydrates	11 g Fat
5 g Saturated Fat	0 mg Cholesterol
71 mg Sodium	5 g Fiber

BRAIN BOOSTERS
50 best brain foods: asparagus, spinach
Brain healthy spices: garlic, sage

LUNCH

EINSTEIN BURGER

◆ **4 - 6 Servings** ◆ **405 Calories** ◆ **8 Brain Boosters**

Ingredients:

1 cup quinoa or brown rice cooked according to directions

1 tablespoon refined coconut oil for mixing

1 tablespoon refined coconut oil for sautéing, or 2-3 tablespoons vegetable broth

1 small sweet onion, chopped

1 carrot, chopped (use organic so you don't have to peel it)

1 clove garlic, minced

1 teaspoon Real Salt

1 teaspoon fresh rosemary, chopped

1 teaspoon fresh thyme, chopped

¼ cup cilantro or handful spinach (depending on desired flavor)

1 tablespoon Bragg Liquid Aminos

¼ teaspoon pepper

½ cup rolled oats

2 cups soaked, cooked beans of your choice (experimenting with the beans changes the flavor of the burger)

Optional: Use canned organic beans in a pinch.

This recipe takes some time to prepare, but can be prepared in advance so it is ready to heat up on the go. For those of you who just have to have a burger, this is the guiltless way to go! I prefer eating the burger without the bun and serve it over a bed of fresh greens or wrapped in a couple leafs of romaine lettuce. Try preparing a few extras and freezing them for future use.

Preparation:

1. First prepare the quinoa or brown rice according to directions on package. This will take 30-40 minutes.
2. In a medium skillet, heat oil or vegetable broth over medium heat. Sauté onions and carrot for 3 minutes. Add garlic and sauté for additional minute. I prefer my veggies not to be very cooked. You can cook them longer if you choose; up to 7 minutes.
3. Add salt, rosemary, thyme, and spinach or cilantro. Cook no longer than 1 minute.
4. Blend oats in a food processor until course and powdery. Transfer to a large mixing bowl and set aside.
5. Put vegetables, beans, and quinoa or rice in the food processor. Pulse lightly until mixture is coarse and holds together, but not mushy. Add mixture to oats and rice and blend well by hand.
6. Form mixture into patties and set on a cooking board. You should be able to get 4-6 patties out of the mixture.

♦ **4 - 6 Servings** ♦ **405 Calories** ♦ **8 Brain Boosters**

Ingredients continued:

Veganaise, as desired
4-6 Ezekiel sprouted grain ham
burger buns
Sliced vegetable toppings, as
desired
1 avocado, sliced
Sprouts
Sunflower seeds

*Optional: Try wrapping the bur-
ger*

Preparation Continued:

7. Cook over medium heat until lightly browned, about 5 minutes each side. If you prefer, you may cook a little longer or "over-sear" them over higher heat for a minute then reduce heat until burgers have a slightly crisp crust, which will make them hold together better. Veggie burgers have a tendency to fall apart easily.

8. Spread Veganaise on Ezekiel buns and lace burgers on bun. Top with a variety of fresh vegetables, avocado, sprouts, and sunflower seeds.

BRAIN BOOSTERS
50 best brain foods: carrots, oats, beans, avocado, vegetables
Brain healthy spices: garlic, rosemary, thyme

USE YOUR HEAD WHEN CHOOSING LETTUCE:
Whenever you see "lettuce" listed as an ingredient in a recipe, choose varieties with the most nutritional value. In this recipe, romaine is preferable to iceberg because it has more nutritional value.

Nutrition Per Serving	
405 Calories	17 g Protein
62 g Carbohydrates	13 g Fat
5 g Saturated Fat	0 mg Cholesterol
237 mg Sodium	14 g Fiber

VEGGIE WRAPS WITH ROASTED CAULIFLOWER

♦ **4 Servings** ♦ **467 Calories** ♦ **4 Brain Boosters**

Ingredients:

2 avocados

1 cucumber, thinly sliced, lengthwise

4 Ezekiel sprouted grain tortillas

1 red bell pepper, diced

½ sweet yellow or red onion, diced

1 tomato, thinly sliced or diced

¼ cup sunflower seeds

Sprouts

Real Salt

Optional: Bragg Liquid Aminos Spray

Optional: hummus

Preparation:

If desired you may heat the tortillas for a couple minutes or they may be eaten cold.

1. Mash avocado in a bowl to a guacamole-like consistency.
2. Cut cucumber in half, then slice thinly, like you would slice cheese.
3. Spread a thin layer of avocado mixture on tortillas in a line.
4. Spread a thin line of hummus on tortilla, if desired.
5. Sprinkle diced veggies.
6. Add cucumber slices, sunflower seeds, and sprouts to each tortilla.
7. Spray lightly with Bragg Liquid Aminos, if desired.
8. Salt to taste.
9. Fold bottom of each wrap up about 2 inches to prevent contents from spilling once rolled.
10. Turn sideways and roll snugly. Be careful not to tear tortillas.

Roasted Cauliflower continued on next page...

Nutrition Per Serving	
467 Calories	15 g Protein
54 g Carbohydrates	25 g Fat
6 g Saturated Fat	0 mg Cholesterol
92 mg Sodium	19 g Fiber

♦ **4 Servings** ♦ **467 Calories** ♦ **4 Brain Boosters**

Roasted Cauliflower Ingredients:

1-2 tablespoons refined coconut oil

1 head cauliflower, cut into florets

¼ cup cilantro, finely chopped

3 garlic cloves, minced

Roasted Cauliflower Preparation:

1. Add cauliflower to boiling water for 2 minutes. Remove from heat and promptly blanch with cold water. Drain well and pat dry.
2. In a medium skillet, heat oil over medium-high heat.
3. Add garlic and cilantro, sauté for 1 minute.
4. Add cauliflower. Stir until florets are coated with garlic and cilantro mixture. Continue cooking and occasionally turning florets until lightly browned, but still crunchy, about 3-5 minutes (less is better).
5. Serve warm.

BRAIN BOOSTERS
50 best brain foods: avocado, red bell pepper, tomatoes
Brain healthy spices: garlic

Nutrition Per Serving, Cauliflower Alone

85 Calories	5 g Protein
12 g Carbohydrates	4 g Fat
0 g Saturated Fat	0 mg Cholesterol
64 mg Sodium	5 g Fiber

♦ 10 Servings ♦ 317 Calories ♦ 9 Brain Boosters

Ingredients:

1 large onion, finely chopped
1 garlic clove, minced
1 leek, finely chopped
2-3 tablespoons vegetable broth
or 1 teaspoon refined coconut oil,
for sautéing onions and garlic
1-2 teaspoons refined coconut oil,
for sautéing mushrooms
1 cup mushrooms, chopped
(preferably wild mushrooms)
2 cups brown rice (pre-cooked in
vegetable broth)
3 stalks celery, finely chopped
1 large carrot, finely chopped
1 cup tomatoes, finely chopped
1 tablespoon fresh basil, finely
chopped
1 tablespoon fresh thyme, finely
chopped (Feel free to experiment
with whatever fresh herbs you
choose. Rosemary and sage are
also excellent choices.)
½ cup whole wheat bread crumbs
1 cup walnuts, finely chopped
½ cup cashews, finely chopped
½ cup almonds, finely chopped
3 eggs (or egg substitute)
¾ cups vegan cheese, grated
1 teaspoon garlic salt
Real Salt and pepper, to taste
Vegetable broth, as needed to
moisten mixture

Advance Preparation:

Cook brown rice while preparing other ingredients.

Preparation:

1. Preheat oven to 425-450 degrees F. It will take a bit longer to cook at the lower temperature, but it will be more moist.

2. Sauté onions, garlic, and leeks over medium heat in a large skillet using either vegetable broth or refined coconut oil for about 2 minutes. If using vegetable broth be sure that excess moisture is evaporated before adding mushrooms. This is one time that coconut oil may be better, but only a small amount is required (maybe a teaspoon or so).

3. Add 1 teaspoon more of coconut oil to sauté pan along with mushrooms. Continue cooking over medium heat until moisture is "sweated" out of the mushrooms and mushrooms begin to brown. This should take 7-10 minutes. Remove from heat and set aside until all other ingredients have been chopped and rice has been cooked.

4. In a large bowl, mix rice, onion, and mushroom mixture, celery, carrot, tomatoes, herbs, bread crumbs, nuts, and garlic salt together.

5. Add egg or egg substitute and vegan cheese to mixture and blend well.

6. Add Real Salt, garlic salt, and pepper as desired.

7. You may either lightly grease a bread pan or line it with wax paper. Put mixture into prepared pan and lightly press into place, smoothing the surface with the back of a spoon.

8. Place in preheated oven for 30-40 minutes depending on temperature. At 450 degrees it should be ready in about 30 minutes. Personally, I prefer the loaf on the "crunchier" side, and it sticks together better when cooked at a slightly higher temp.

9. This nut loaf is fabulous topped with either a marinara sauce or a mushroom sauce, found on the next page.

◆ **10 Servings** ◆ **317 Calories** ◆ **9 Brain Boosters**

LUNCH

Wild Mushroom Gravy Ingredients:

1 teaspoon refined coconut oil
1 small onion, finely chopped
1 leek, finely sliced (discard green portion)
1 garlic clove, minced
1 cup wild mushrooms
1 tablespoon flour (or adjust as needed to thicken)
1 cup vegetable broth
¼ cup soy cream
1 teaspoon soy sauce
1 teaspoon Worcestershire sauce
Real Salt and pepper
Optional: 1 tablespoon fresh parsley, chopped

Marinara Sauce Ingredients:

1-2 teaspoons refined coconut oil
½ cup onion, chopped
2 garlic cloves, minced
1 tablespoon fresh oregano, finely chopped
1 tablespoon fresh basil, finely chopped
3 cups tomatoes, peeled and diced (you may used organic canned tomatoes if you desire)
Real Salt and pepper, as desired for flavor
Optional: For a thicker sauce try adding a couple tablespoons of tomato paste.

Wild Mushroom Preparation:

1. Heat coconut oil in medium skillet over medium heat. Sauté onions, leek, and garlic for 2-3 minutes. Add mushrooms and sauté until browned, about 10 minutes.
2. Add flour to absorb moisture from mushrooms.
3. Stir in broth, cream, spices, soy sauce, Worcestershire sauce, and parsley. Simmer until thickened and heated through.
4. Add salt and pepper to taste.

Marinara Sauce Preparation:

1. Heat oil in a large pan over medium heat. Add onions and sauté for about 2 minutes.
2. Add garlic and sauté for about another minute.
3. Stir in herbs and tomatoes. Reduce heat to low for 8-10 minutes. For thicker sauce, mix in a couple tablespoons of tomato paste. Spoon over nut loaf when ready.

BRAIN BOOSTERS
50 best brain foods: carrots, tomatoes, walnuts, almonds, eggs
Brain healthy spices: garlic, basil, thyme, oregano

Nutrition Per Serving, Roasted Nut Loaf

317 Calories	9 g Protein
25 g Carbohydrates	22 g Fat
3 g Saturated Fat	63 mg Cholesterol
113 mg Sodium	5 g Fiber

Nutrition Per Serving, Mushroom Gravy Alone

55 Calories	3 g Protein
9 g Carbohydrates	1 g Fat
1 g Saturated Fat	63 mg Cholesterol
624 mg Sodium	1 g Fiber

Nutrition Per Serving, Marinara Sauce Alone

46 Calories	2 g Protein
8 g Carbohydrates	2 g Fat
1 g Saturated Fat	63 mg Cholesterol
8 mg Sodium	2 g Fiber

◆ **4 Servings** ◆ **215 Calories** ◆ **4 Brain Boosters**

Ingredients:

1 large can tuna or 12 ounces fresh ahi, cooked and ground or finely chopped

2 tablespoons Veganaise

2 large red bell peppers

1 cucumber, thinly sliced

1 tomato, sliced

¼ cup sweet onion, diced

1 avocado

¼ - ½ cup sprouts

Real Salt and pepper

Optional: Bragg Liquid Aminos Spray

Optional: Spice up tuna by adding chopped celery, onion, and 1 tablespoon Dijon mustard.

This is a great lunch if you are "on the run." It is quick, nutritious, and filling when you don't have time to prepare anything more elaborate… and it beats fast food!

Preparation:

1. Put drained tuna into medium bowl. Add Veganaise and mix well. Add celery, onion, and mustard if desired.
2. Gently cut tops off bell peppers. Carefully slice peppers in half, making sure the peppers have enough room to hold the tuna and veggies. If the peppers are small, you may have to cut out a smaller section (less than half) and retain the larger piece. The peppers should maintain a "boat" shape. Clean out the seeds and wash the peppers.
3. Cut cucumber in half, then standing each half on end, cut into thin slices (like cheese slices). Set aside.
4. Slice tomato and set aside.
5. Avocado may be sliced or scooped into a bowl and smashed with a fork to make a spread. I prefer making it into a spread.
6. Place a layer of avocado spread in red bell pepper boats. If using avocado slices, add at the end.
7. Spread a layer of tuna over the avocado.
8. Add cucumber slices, tomato slices, and sprouts.
9. Sprinkle with salt and pepper to taste. Spray with Bragg Liquid Aminos Spray. Serve cold.

BRAIN BOOSTERS
50 best brain foods: tuna, red bell peppers, tomatoes, avocado

Nutrition Per Serving	
215 Calories	13 g Protein
14 g Carbohydrates	12 g Fat
2 g Saturated Fat	13 mg Cholesterol
75 mg Sodium	6 g Fiber

VITAL VEGETABLE CREPES

♦ **6 Servings** ♦ **206 Calories** ♦ **6 Brain Boosters**

Ingredients:

½ cup Egg Beaters

½ cup almond milk, unsweetened

⅔ cup buckwheat flour, or spelt flour

1-2 teaspoons refined coconut oil

Note: This recipe can be done one of two ways. If time allows, you can grill the vegetables for an awesome taste. But for a quick and healthy alternative, this is also great with raw vegetables. Be creative. Here are a couple of suggestions.

Grilled Vegetables Ingredients:

2 tablespoons refined coconut oil

1 yellow squash, sliced lengthwise

1 zucchini, sliced lengthwise

8 green onions

½ eggplant, sliced

1 cup hummus or baba ghanoush

Optional: 1 avocado, sliced

Preparation:

1. In a medium mixing bowl, blend Egg Beaters, almond milk, and flour. Mix well.
2. Heat oil in a medium skillet over medium heat.
3. Pour ¼ of the batter into the skillet. Quickly spread the batter across the skillet by lifting and turning until the batter spreads evenly. When the edges of the crepe begin to brown and lift, carefully lift and flip the crepe. Cook until both sides are lightly browned, about 2 minutes.
4. Place each crepe on a plate as they are finished. Add a little more oil as necessary for remaining crepes.
5. Spoon hummus or baba ghanoush into center of crepe, top with grilled or fresh vegetables and fold in half. Place avocado wedges on top if desired.

Preparation for grilled vegetables:

1. Preheat grill to medium-high or oven to 400 degrees F. In a large bag or bowl mix 2 tablespoons refined coconut oil (warmed), 1 teaspoon Real Salt and ½ teaspoon pepper.
2. Add vegetables and lightly coat.
3. If grilling vegetables place on grill and turn frequently. Do not leave unattended. Grill until vegetables are tender but crisp. I prefer my vegetables crunchy, about 8-10 minutes.
4. If roasting vegetables in oven, lightly oil a cookie sheet and place vegetables on sheet. Bake for 8-10 minutes. Turn at least once. Check to be sure vegetables are not getting scorched. Add to crepes.

Raw vegetables option:

Use 2 cups of mixed vegetables of your choice. Top with sprouts.

BRAIN BOOSTERS

50 best brain foods: eggs, almond milk, garbanzo beans (in the hummus), avocado, red bell peppers, broccoli

Nutrition Per Serving

206 Calories	6 g Protein
22 g Carbohydrates	12 g Fat
0 g Saturated Fat	7 mg Cholesterol
52 mg Sodium	5 g Fiber

STIMULATING STIR-FRY

♦ **4 Servings** ♦ **190 Calories** ♦ **7 Brain Boosters**

Ingredients:

1 tablespoon corn starch

1 tablespoon low-sodium soy sauce

1 tablespoon sesame oil

½ cup cold water

¼ cup vegetable broth or 2 teaspoons refined coconut oil, for sautéing

2 garlic cloves, minced

1 tablespoon ginger, finely grated

1 14-ounce package firm or very firm tofu for vegetarians

Optional: 1 pound peeled and de veined shrimp for non-vegetarians

1 cup carrots

1 cup broccoli florets

½ cup mushrooms, sliced

1 cup bok choy, thinly chopped

½ cup snow peas

¼ cup bean sprouts

2 green onions, cut into 2-inch pieces

Optional: ¼ cup almonds, shaved

Preparation:

1. In advance, prepare sauce. Mix corn starch, soy sauce, sesame oil, and water. Blend well and set aside.
2. Heat the vegetable broth or water in a nonstick wok or large skillet over medium heat. If not using a nonstick wok (or if you are adding tofu or shrimp), you may have to use unrefined coconut oil for sautéing.
3. Add ginger and garlic, sauté for about 1 minute.
4. Add either tofu or shrimp and stir for about 1 minute.
5. Add carrots and broccoli, sauté for about 1 minute.
6. Add mushrooms and bok choy, sauté for an additional 2 minutes.
7. Add snow peas, sprouts, and green onions last, sauté for about 1 minute.
8. Add sauce and mix into vegetables until thickened for about 10-20 seconds.
9. Serve hot. You may choose to serve over brown rice or barley.

BRAIN BOOSTERS
50 best brain foods: water, tofu, carrots, broccoli, almonds
Brain healthy spices: garlic, ginger

Nutrition Per Serving with Shrimp	
190 Calories	26 g Protein
10 g Carbohydrates	5 g Fat
1 g Saturated Fat	221 mg Cholesterol
496 mg Sodium	2 g Fiber

Nutrition Per Serving with Tofu	
156 Calories	11 g Protein
12 g Carbohydrates	8 g Fat
1 g Saturated Fat	0 mg Cholesterol
277 mg Sodium	3 g Fiber

♦ **4 Servings** ♦ **76 Calories** ♦ **4 Brain Boosters**

Ingredients:

2 eggplants
1 garlic clove, chopped
1 tablespoon lemon juice
2 tablespoon tahini
½ teaspoon Real Salt
½ teaspoon cumin
2 tablespoons extra virgin olive
oil

*Optional: 1 tablespoon pine nuts
and 3-4 olives*

Preparation:

1. Poke eggplant with fork on all sides and then grill eggplant until it is charred on all sides.
2. Scoop out insides of eggplant and put into blender with all other ingredients. Blend until smooth and creamy.
3. Place into decorative serving bowl.

Optional: Sprinkle with pine nuts and olives.

BRAIN BOOSTERS
50 best brain foods: olives, olive oil
Brain healthy spices: garlic, cinnamon

Nutrition Per Serving

76 Calories	2 g Protein
11 g Carbohydrates	4 g Fat
1 g Saturated Fat	13 mg Cholesterol
285 mg Sodium	4 g Fiber

LUNCH

GRILLED ARTICHOKES & NUTTED COUSCOUS

♦ **8 Servings** ♦ **585 Calories** ♦ **6 Brain Boosters**

Ingredients:

4 artichokes
1 tablespoon fresh lemon juice
¼ cup melted ghee or refined coconut oil
3 garlic cloves, minced
1 teaspoon Real Salt
½ teaspoon pepper

Nutted Couscous Ingredients:

1 cup asparagus tips
2 cups instant couscous
2 cups vegetable broth
3 tablespoons Earth Balance
¼ cup fresh mint, finely chopped
¼ cup pine nuts

Optional: ¼ cup currants

Optional: 1 cup shrimp, cooked (thawed) or 8 ounces firm tofu

Artichokes Preparation:

1. Preheat outdoor grill to medium-high heat.
2. Fill a large pot of water halfway and bring it to a boil. While waiting for water to boil, prepare artichokes.
3. Turn artichokes on their sides. With a large knife cut the stem off close to the base of the artichoke so that it sits upright. Then chop the top 1 inch of each artichoke. With a pair of scissors quickly trim the tips of each leaf to rid the artichokes of pointed tips. Cut artichokes in half.
4. Add artichokes to boiling water for 20 minutes.
5. Drain water from artichokes and turn artichokes upside down to remove excess water.
6. In a small sauce bowl mix lemon juice, melted ghee or coconut oil, garlic, salt, and pepper.
7. Lightly brush all sides of artichokes with oil mixture and place on the grill.
8. Turn frequently and brush the rest of the mixture on the artichokes.
9. Grill until tips of leaves are slightly charred.

Nutted Couscous continued on next page...

Nutrition Per Serving, Whole Recipe	
585 Calories	15 g Protein
66 g Carbohydrates	30 g Fat
10 g Saturated Fat	17 mg Cholesterol
1486 mg Sodium	13 g Fiber

Nutrition Per Serving, Nutted Couscous	
223 Calories	6 g Protein
33 g Carbohydrates	7 g Fat
2 g Saturated Fat	0 mg Cholesterol
288 mg Sodium	3 g Fiber

♦ **8 Servings** ♦ **585 Calories** ♦ **6 Brain Boosters**

Nutted Couscous Preparation:

1. In a medium saucepan bring a small amount of water to a boil. Using a steamer basket, steam asparagus tips for about 5-7 minutes. Do not allow water to bathe asparagus.
2. Meanwhile, in another medium saucepan, bring vegetable broth and Earth Balance to a boil. Remove from heat. Add couscous and let stand for 5 minutes.
3. Dump couscous into a serving bowl. Add asparagus tips, mint, pine nuts, and currants if desired. Lightly turn until mixed well.
4. If adding shrimp, quickly heat 1 tablespoon refined coconut oil over medium heat and sauté shrimp for 3 or 4 minutes. Add to the top of couscous. If adding tofu, heat 1 tablespoon refined coconut oil over medium heat. Sauté tofu for about 5 minutes, until warmed through and slightly browned. Add spices and herbs as desired. A couple of pressed garlic cloves really help add a lot of flavor to tofu.
5. Serve warm.

SERVING SUGGESTION: *Hummus and raw veggies (page 95).*

BRAIN BOOSTERS, WHOLE RECIPE
50 best brain foods: asparagus, tofu, red bell pepper, garbanzo beans (in the hummus), olive oil
Brain healthy spices: garlic

Nutrition Per Serving, Artichokes Alone	
178 Calories	3 g Protein
10 g Carbohydrates	15 g Fat
8 g Saturated Fat	16 mg Cholesterol
637 mg Sodium	5 g Fiber

LUNCH

♦ **8 Servings** ♦ **179 Calories** ♦ **4 Brain Boosters**

Fresh Vegetables Ingredients:

1 red bell pepper, sliced
½ head of cauliflower, cut into florets
2 celery stalks, cut into 3-inch pieces
1 cucumber, cut in half, and sliced lengthwise
½ cup hummus

Hummus Ingredients:

2 garlic cloves
2 cups garbanzo beans, cooked (use organic canned beans if you prefer)
½ cup lemon juice
¼ cup tahini paste
1 teaspoon Real Salt
1 teaspoon cumin
2 tablespoons extra virgin olive oil
Paprika, for garnish

Vegetable Preparation:

Prepare vegetables in advance. Arrange vegetables on a platter with hummus in the center.

Hummus Preparation:

1. Place garlic in food processor and pulse several times.
2. Add garbanzo beans and lemon juice. Pulse several more times.
3. Add tahini, salt, and cumin. Blend until mixture is smooth.
4. While mixing, continuously add olive oil in a steady stream for even, smooth blending of ingredients.
5. Transfer to a serving bowl and lightly dust with paprika.

BRAIN BOOSTERS FOR HUMMUS ONLY
50 best brain foods: red bell pepper, garbanzo beans (in the hummus), olive oil
Brain healthy spices: garlic

Nutrition Per Serving, Hummus & Veggies	
179 Calories	8 g Protein
28 g Carbohydrates	6 g Fat
1 g Saturated Fat	16 mg Cholesterol
401 mg Sodium	9 g Fiber

Nutrition Per Serving, Hummus Alone	
223 Calories	6 g Protein
33 g Carbohydrates	7 g Fat
2 g Saturated Fat	0 mg Cholesterol
288 mg Sodium	3 g Fiber

♦ **6 Servings** ♦ **704 Calories** ♦ **7 Brain Boosters**

Ingredients:
1 head cauliflower, cut into florets
2 cups vegetable broth or water
¼ cup almond milk, unsweetened
1 tablespoon Earth Balance
½ teaspoon Italian seasoning
2 garlic cloves, minced
1 teaspoon fresh rosemary, chopped
2 teaspoons cornstarch mixed with 2 tablespoons water
Real Salt and pepper, to taste
2 cups baby spinach leaves
¼ cup sunflower seeds

Optional: 2 tablespoons chives, finely Chopped

Grilled Vegetables:
1 bunch asparagus
1 red bell pepper, sliced
2 zucchini, sliced lengthwise
2 yellow squash, sliced lengthwise
Optional: 2 Portobello mushrooms, sliced
½ cup refined coconut oil
Optional ¼ cup vinegar (I prefer it without)
1 teaspoon Real Salt
½ teaspoon pepper

Cauliflower Mashed "Potatoes" Preparation:

1. Pour vegetable broth into a medium pot. Put cauliflower florets in pot and bring to a boil over medium-high heat. Cover, reduce heat to low, and simmer for 10 minutes.

2. If you prefer using water, then steam cauliflower in a steamer basket being sure not to allow the water to bathe the cauliflower. If steaming, cook until fork tender, about 8 minutes.

3. While cauliflower is cooking, combine almond milk, Earth Balance, garlic, Italian seasoning, and rosemary in a small saucepan over medium heat. When it reaches a boil add the cornstarch/water mixture, STIRRING CONSTANTLY until it is thickened and smooth. Remove from heat and set aside.

4. Drain as much liquid from cauliflower as possible and place florets in a food processor or blender, blending on high for about 1 minute. Add sauce and blend until smooth and creamy.

5. Spice with salt and pepper to taste.

6. Add sunflower seeds and chives if desired.

7. Serve hot over a bed of spinach.

Grilled Vegetables Preparation: See page 89.

BRAIN BOOSTERS
50 best brain foods: water, almond milk, spinach, asparagus, red bell pepper
Brain healthy spices: garlic, rosemary

Nutrition Per Serving, Whole Recipe	
704 Calories	13 g Protein
36 g Carbohydrates	63 g Fat
49 g Saturated Fat	0 mg Cholesterol
594 mg Sodium	13 g Fiber

Nutrition Per Serving, Mashed Only	
435 Calories	10 g Protein
29 g Carbohydrates	35 g Fat
25 g Saturated Fat	0 mg Cholesterol
590 mg Sodium	11 g Fiber

CHAPTER 7

Brain Sustaining Dinners

Dinner needs to be healthy and filling but relatively light, so that the food does not just sit in your system. Plus, you need to leave a little room for dessert.

DINNER

SMART BRAIN SPAGHETTI

♦ **4 Servings** ♦ **139 Calories** ♦ **5 Brain Boosters**

Ingredients:

1 large spaghetti squash
1 tablespoon refined coconut oil
1 small yellow onion, chopped
1-2 garlic cloves, minced or pressed
½ cup zucchini, chopped
½ cup red bell pepper, chopped
4 medium vine-ripened tomatoes, diced
1 8-ounce can tomato sauce
1½ tablespoons fresh basil, finely chopped (or 1 tablespoon dried)
1½ tablespoons fresh oregano, finely chopped (or 1 tablespoon dried)
1 tablespoon tomato paste, dissolved in ¼ cup vegetable broth or water
¼ teaspoon pepper
1 tablespoon Real Salt
Optional: 1/2 cup mushrooms, sliced
Optional: For thicker sauce add 1 teaspoon corn starch dissolved in ¼ cup soy creamer at the end.

Preparation:

1. Preheat oven to 375 degrees F.
2. Cut spaghetti squash in half. Clean out seeds. Place squash face down on a baking dish and place in oven for about 45 minutes.
3. While squash is baking heat oil in a large skillet and sauté onions, garlic, and zucchini for 3 minutes over medium heat.
4. Add red bell pepper and mushrooms, sauté for 1 minute.
5. Add remaining ingredients, except water, and simmer over low heat until squash is finished.
6. Monitor sauce for consistency to determine amount of water to be added. Add as needed.
7. If you prefer a slightly thicker consistency to your sauce add the cornstarch dissolved in soy cream now. It won't really change the flavor much, but it will thicken it a bit.
8. When squash is finished, let cool for 5 minutes. Use a fork to scoop out the spaghetti squash into a bowl. Squash is finished when the fork goes in easily. Squash shreds like spaghetti.
9. Spoon sauce over "spaghetti" and serve hot.

BRAIN BOOSTERS
50 best brain foods: red bell pepper, tomatoes
Brain healthy spices: garlic, basil, oregano

Nutrition Per Serving	
139 Calories	4 g Protein
25 g Carbohydrates	4 g Fat
3 g Saturated Fat	7 mg Cholesterol
2046 mg Sodium	7 g Fiber

♦ **4 Servings** ♦ **195 Calories** ♦ **4 Brain Boosters**

DINNER

Ingredients:

1 tablespoon coconut oil or 3-4 tablespoons vegetable broth, for sautéing

3 garlic cloves, minced

1 tablespoon tomato paste

2¾ cups vegetable broth

2 teaspoons fresh tarragon, chopped

1 teaspoon saffron

2-inch sliced orange peel, or large piece orange zest

1 bay leaf

1½ cup organic tomatoes, stewed or diced

½ cup fennel

1 leek (white only), sliced

½ cup okra, sliced

Real Salt and pepper, to taste

4 tilapia fillets

4 lemon wedges

Preparation:

1. Heat oil in large skillet over medium heat. Add garlic and sauté for 1 minute.
2. Add tomato paste and sauté for one minute. Deglaze skillet with 1 cup vegetable broth.
3. Add tarragon, saffron, orange zest, and bay leaf. Simmer for 15 minutes.
4. Remove bay leaf and orange zest. Add tomato and vegetable broth. Bring to a boil.
5. Add leek, fennel, and okra. Simmer until vegetables are tender.
6. Season fish with salt and pepper. Add fish to sauce and gently poach for 3-4 minutes each side.
7. Serve immediately in shallow dishes. Garnish each dish with one lemon wedge.

Vegetarian option: For those who do not eat animal protein of any kind, this sauce is also excellent served over barley.

BRAIN BOOSTERS
50 best brain foods: orange, tomatoes
Brain healthy spices: garlic, saffron

Nutrition Per Serving

195 Calories	23 g Protein
18 g Carbohydrates	5 g Fat
4 g Saturated Fat	55 mg Cholesterol
914 mg Sodium	4 g Fiber

◆ **8 Servings** ◆ **209 Calories** ◆ **5 Brain Boosters**

Ingredients:

1 tablespoon refined coconut oil

1 pound lean ground turkey (free range, hormone free)

1 cup chopped onion

3 garlic cloves, chopped

1 teaspoon chili powder

1 small can Ortega chilis

1 tablespoon fresh oregano

1 teaspoon cumin seed

1-2 teaspoons Real Salt

3 cups diced tomatoes, fresh or organic canned (no-salt-added variety)

2 cups chicken or vegetable broth

2 cups celery, chopped

1 cup bell peppers, chopped

1/2 cup zucchini, chopped

2 cups kidney beans, cooked and drained (you may use canned if you don't have time to cook beans)

1 cup black beans or chickpea beans, cooked

Optional: 1 jalapeno pepper (makes chili pretty spicy)

Preparation:

1. Note: It is my preference to cook the vegetables as little as possible. As a result you will be blending them in step 4. However, if you prefer not go through the process of blending the vegetables, and prefer cooking the vegetables, you will need to sauté them as step 1. In that case, heat a teaspoon of refined coconut oil in a large skillet over medium heat for about 1 minute. Add bell pepper and celery, sauté for about 2 minutes. Then proceed to step 2.

2. In a large saucepan or pot, brown turkey meat in refined coconut oil over medium heat. Crumble turkey and break apart as much as possible. Add onion and stir for about 2 minutes.

3. Add garlic, jalapeno (if using), chili powder, Ortega chilis, oregano, cumin seed, salt, and tomatoes. Mix thoroughly until spices are well blended with meat and meat is browned (no longer pink).

4. Add broth.

5. *Optional: Dish out 2 cups of chili mixture. Put about one cup of chili at a time into the blender. Add ½ cup of chopped bell pepper, zucchini, and celery at a time and purée. Pour mixture back into the remaining chili pot. Adding the puréed vegetables not only makes the chili tasty, but is a great way to add fiber and vitamins without overcooking.*

6. Add beans. Stir thoroughly and heat through on medium-low, about 5 minutes. Serve hot.

BRAIN BOOSTERS
50 best brain foods: turkey, tomatoes, bell peppers, black beans
Brain healthy spices: garlic

Nutrition Per Serving

209 Calories	22 g Protein
24 g Carbohydrates	4 g Fat
2 g Saturated Fat	7 mg Cholesterol
687 mg Sodium	8 g Fiber

◆ **6 Servings** ◆ **150 Calories** ◆ **7 Brain Boosters**

Ingredients:

1 tablespoon refined coconut oil

1 onion, diced

2 garlic cloves, minced

4 Boca burgers (for vegetarians)

1 tablespoon chili powder

1 small can Ortega chilis

1 tablespoon fresh oregano

1-2 teaspoons Real Salt

3 cups tomatoes, peeled, deseeded, and diced (you may use strained tomatoes from a can if you don't have time to peel and deseed fresh tomatoes).

1 cup vegetable broth

1 cup kidney beans, cooked (you may use canned if you don't have time to cook beans)

1 cup black beans or chickpea beans, cooked

3 cups mixed vegetables: ½ cup red bell pepper, ½ cup yellow bell pepper, ½ cup carrots, ½ cup zucchini, ½ cup squash, ½ cup crumbled cauliflower. Be creative! If you prefer other vegetables, feel free to add them.

Optional: 1 jalapeno pepper (makes chili pretty spicy)

Preparation:

1. In a large saucepan or pot, heat oil over medium heat. Sauté onions and garlic for about 2 minutes.
2. Add Boca burgers. Crumble and brown burgers, breaking apart as much as possible.
3. Add jalapeno (if using), chili powder, Ortega chilis, oregano, salt, and tomatoes. Mix thoroughly until spices are well blended.
4. Add broth.
5. Dish out 2 cups of chili mixture. Put about one cup of chili at a time into the blender. Add ¾ cups of vegetables at a time and purée. Pour mixture back into the remaining chili pot. Add beans. Stir thoroughly and heat through on medium-low, about 5 minutes. Serve hot.

BRAIN BOOSTERS
50 best brain foods: tomatoes, black beans, red bell peppers, yellow bell peppers, carrots
Brain healthy spices: garlic, oregano

Nutrition Per Serving	
150 Calories	12 g Protein
23 g Carbohydrates	3 g Fat
2 g Saturated Fat	7 mg Cholesterol
580 g Sodium	8 g Fiber

STUFFED VEGETABLES

◆ **10 Servings** ◆ **317 Calories** ◆ **5 Brain Boosters**

Ingredients For Filling:

1 pound lean ground lamb (grass fed, hormone free). Lamb can be substituted with beef.
Vegetarian option: Substitute meat for a blend of mushrooms and ground walnuts (blend in food processor for fine consistency)
1½ cups barley or brown rice, cooked
3 cups onion, chopped
½ cup Italian parsley, chopped
¼ cup fresh mint, chopped
¼ cup fresh lemon juice
2 tablespoons fresh minced sage
2 tablespoons garlic, minced
2 tablespoons marjoram, minced
2 teaspoons Real Salt
1 teaspoon black pepper
2 tablespoons tomato paste
2 cups tomatoes, finely chopped
Put vegetables in food processor on "pulse" mode for a "finely chopped" consistency. Do not over-process.

Vegetables for Stuffing:

4 large red bell peppers
3 zucchinis, halved lengthwise
4 Japanese eggplants, halved lengthwise
3 yellow crookneck squash, halved lengthwise

Optional: Boil cabbage and use cabbage leaves to cover the bottom of baking dish for stuffed vegetables to be placed on.

Preparation for filling:

1. If making vegetarian version, chop mushrooms and sauté in 1 tablespoon refined coconut oil. You may sauté the onions and garlic with the mushrooms if desired.
2. For meat version mix onion, garlic, and bell pepper in a food processor.
3. Add rice, meat or mushroom mix, herbs, spices, and tomato paste. Pulse until well blended.
4. Add tomatoes last and mix in gently.
5. Cover stuffing mixture and refrigerate until vegetables are prepared for stuffing.

To prepare vegetables to be stuffed:

1. Use a small, sharp knife to carefully shave away the core of the eggplants, zucchini, and yellow squash. Make the shells about ⅛-inch thick. Do not pierce the skins.
2. Cut the tops off the red bell peppers. Scoop out the inner seeds and flesh. Rinse well. Set the tops of the peppers aside.
3. Spoon the filling into the vegetable shells and arrange vegetables in baking dish or roasting pan.

BRAIN BOOSTERS
50 best brain foods: tomatoes, red bell peppers
Brain healthy spices: sage, garlic, marjoram

Nutrition Per Serving	
317 Calories	16 g Protein
42 g Carbohydrates	11 g Fat
4 g Saturated Fat	30 mg Cholesterol
529 mg Sodium	13 g Fiber

♦   **10 Servings**   ♦   **317 Calories**   ♦   **5 Brain Boosters**

Broth Ingredients:

3 tablespoons Earth Balance butter substitute or refined coconut oil

1 tablespoon shallot, minced

1 tablespoon dried mint, crushed

¼ cup tomato paste

2 cups vegetable broth

Broth Preparation:

1. Preheat oven to 350 degrees F.
2. Melt Earth Balance or refined coconut oil in a heavy, medium-size sauce pan over medium-high heat until it starts to sizzle. Stir in shallot and mint.
3. Stir in tomato paste.
4. Add broth and bring to a boil.
5. Pour broth over vegetables.
6. Cover roasting pan with foil and place in preheated oven. Bake vegetables until tender; about 1 hour.
7. Allow to cool for about 10 minutes prior to serving. Dish onto plates or shallow bowls and spoon broth over the top.

GINGER GLAZED SALMON

♦　**4 Servings**　♦　**246 Calories**　♦　**2 Brain Boosters**

Ingredients:

2 8-ounce salmon fillets

2 tablespoons honey

1 tablespoon fresh lemon juice

1 tablespoon low-sodium soy sauce

2 tablespoons ginger root, finely grated

1 tablespoon Dijon mustard

Preparation:

1. In a small mixing bowl, combine honey, lemon juice, soy sauce, ginger root, and mustard. Mix well. Transfer mixture to a shallow baking dish and spread mixture out.
2. Place salmon fillets in baking dish and coat one side of fillets with marinade. Turn fillets over and coat the other side. Cover and marinate for 20-30 minutes, turning occasionally.
3.   Preheat grill to medium heat. Grill fillets for 4-5 minutes on each side depending on thickness. Cut the fillets in half.
4. *Optional: Salmon may also be cooked in a pan over medium heat. It does not fall apart as easily and remains very moist. However, it loses the "grilled" flavor.*
5. Serve immediately.

SERVING SUGGESTION: *Ginger glazed salmon goes wonderfully with Cucumber Edamame Salad (page 45) and grilled asparagus.*

BRAIN BOOSTERS
50 best brain foods: salmon
Brain healthy spices: ginger

Nutrition Per Serving	
246 Calories	29 g Protein
5 g Carbohydrates	9 g Fat
1 g Saturated Fat	80 mg Cholesterol
245 mg Sodium	0 g Fiber

SIMPLY TASTY, HEALTHY SEA BASS

♦ **4 Servings** ♦ **155 Calories** ♦ **Gluten-Free**

DINNER

Ingredients:

2 sea bass fillets, 6-8 ounces each
2-3 tablespoons Earth Balance or butter (they used butter)
Real Salt and pepper, to taste

I admit that I struggled with sea bass recipes for years. I was never very good at cooking fish. I thought it was because I hadn't found the "right" recipe. Of course, the right recipe must have some really special ingredients and require some secret preparation, or I would have learned it by now. One night my husband and I were having dinner at one of the nicest fish restaurants in Orange County. Sea Bass was their specialty. I decided to ask them how they prepare it, as it is clearly the best around, and I was shocked! Here it is…

Preparation:

1. Preheat broiler.
2. Melt Earth Balance or butter in small glass dish. This is one time you may want to use butter because it is more stable for cooking at high temperatures. You may use ghee, which is clarified butter, but it has a different flavor.
3. Preheat a small skillet that has no handle (can be transferred from the stove top to the oven) on the stove top on moderately high heat. Make sure it is hot before you start and have the stove top fan going or a window open.
4. Place the fillets in a dish. Use a basting brush to baste both sides of fillets with melted Earth Balance.
5. When skillet is hot quickly place fillets on heated surface for 1 minute per side, including sides of fish. You may have to use tongs for this.
6. Immediately transfer fish and skillet directly to preheated oven (on broil setting).
7. Broil for 3-4 minutes (depending on size). Turn fillets and broil for another 3-4 minutes.
8. Test fish before serving.

Optional: As an alternative, try using the tomato broth with fennel from the Poached Tilapia in Saffron Sauce (page 103).

SERVING SUGGESTION: *Cut the fillets in half and serve over a bed of steamed, spiced spinach with a Pomegranate Walnut Salad (page 50). Yum!*

Nutrition Per Serving

155 Calories	20 g Protein
0 g Carbohydrates	8 g Fat
3 g Saturated Fat	45 mg Cholesterol
134 mg Sodium	0 g Fiber

♦ **6 Servings** ♦ **124 Calories** ♦ **7 Brain Boosters**

Ingredients:

1 medium eggplant, peeled and cubed
1 onion, chopped
½ cup green beans
1 small zucchini, sliced
1 cup asparagus, chopped
2 garlic cloves, very thinly sliced
3-4 medium tomatoes
2 cups spinach
1 red bell pepper, thinly sliced
2 tablespoons refined coconut oil or 3-4 tablespoons vegetable broth, for sautéing
2 tablespoons fresh Italian parsley, chopped
1 teaspoon fresh thyme, finely chopped (or ½ teaspoon dry)
2 teaspoons fresh basil, finely chopped (or 1 teaspoon dry)
1 teaspoon onion powder
½ teaspoon garlic powder
½ cup white beans
2 cups cooked barley
Real Salt and pepper, to taste

Advance Preparation:

Cook barley according to instructions. Barley usually takes about 35 minutes to simmer.

Preparation:

1. In a large skillet, over medium heat, lightly sauté all vegetables, except spinach and parsley, in vegetable broth or refined coconut oil for 2-4 minutes.
2. Stir in thyme, parsley, basil, onion powder, garlic powder, salt, and pepper.
3. Simmer on low heat for a few minutes to allow flavors to marry.
4. Mix in beans.
5. Add spinach and stir for 30 seconds.
6. Serve over barley.

Optional: If you need more protein, try adding cubes of seitan (for vegetarians) or serving over grilled fish.

BRAIN BOOSTERS

50 best brain foods: asparagus, tomatoes, spinach, red bell pepper
Brain healthy spices: garlic, thyme, basil

Nutrition Per Serving

124 Calories	5 g Protein
18 g Carbohydrates	5 g Fat
4 g Saturated Fat	7 mg Cholesterol
20 mg Sodium	7 g Fiber

♦ **4 Servings** ♦ **172 Calories** ♦ **4 Brain Boosters**

Ingredients:

2 large sea bass fillets (8-10 ounces)

1 tablespoon refined coconut oil

½ onion, chopped

2 garlic cloves, minced

1 teaspoon ground coriander

¼ teaspoon cayenne pepper

½ teaspoon Real Salt

2 fennel bulbs, quartered and sliced lengthwise

¼ teaspoon cinnamon

1 14-ounce can whole tomatoes

2 cups vegetable broth

1 cup water

Preparation:

Prepare sea bass in advance by rinsing with cold water and patting dry with paper towels. Set aside.

1. Heat oil in large pan over medium heat. Sauté onion and garlic for about 3 minutes.
2. Stir in coriander, salt, pepper, and cinnamon.
3. Add tomatoes, broth, and water.
4. Add fennel when broth comes to a boil.
5. Reduce heat to low and simmer for 5 minutes.
6. Place sea bass in sauce. Increase heat to medium for 5-6 minutes. Turn fish over and cover pan. Allow fish to poach for another 5-6 minutes.
7. Carefully cut both fillets in half and place in shallow bowls.
8. Spoon sauce over the top of each fillet and serve hot.

BRAIN BOOSTERS
50 best brain foods: tomatoes, water
Brain healthy spices: garlic, cinnamon

Nutrition Per Serving

172 Calories	15 g Protein
17 g Carbohydrates	6 g Fat
4 g Saturated Fat	27 mg Cholesterol
1039 mg Sodium	5 g Fiber

DINNER

◆　**6 Servings**　◆　**405 Calories**　◆　**5 Brain Boosters**

Ingredients:

4 tablespoons coconut oil
1 tablespoon ground cumin
½ teaspoon paprika
1 teaspoon chili powder
½ teaspoon Real Salt
¼ teaspoon pepper
2 garlic cloves, minced
½ small eggplant, peeled and diced
1 zucchini, sliced
1 yellow squash, sliced
1 red bell pepper, thinly sliced
1 yellow onion, diced
½ cup cilantro, chopped
3 cups shredded lettuce or cabbage
1 cup black or pinto beans
2 ripe avocados, pitted, peeled and mashed (guacamole style)
2 vine-ripened tomatoes, cut into wedges
6 Ezekiel sprouted grain tortillas
Salsa (see recipe below)

Salsa Ingredients:
1 small onion, cut into quarters
2 garlic cloves, cut in half
¼ cup cilantro
1 lime, juiced
½-1 jalapeno (depending on how spicy you like it), roughly chopped. Remove seeds unless you like it *really* hot!
1 28-ounce can whole tomatoes
⅛ teaspoon cayenne pepper
1 teaspoon Real Salt
½ teaspoon pepper

Preparation:

1. Preheat oven to 400 degrees F.   Lightly oil two cookie sheets.
2. In a small bowl mix together oil (may need to be melted), cumin, paprika, chili powder, salt, pepper, and garlic.
3. Place eggplant, zucchini, squash, bell pepper, and onion on cookie sheets and lightly brush with oil mixture.
4. Place in oven and roast for 20-25 minutes or until eggplant is tender. Be sure to turn vegetables at least once.
5. Meanwhile heat tortillas and make salsa. Heat tortillas by wrapping in foil and placing in warm oven for 5-8 minutes. Do not overheat or they will crack and fall apart.
6. Heat beans and place in serving bowl.
7. Arrange vegetables separately on a serving platter and serve hot. Place avocado, tomatoes, and cabbage on a serving tray.
8. Serve warm vegetables, cold vegetables, salsa, and beans together.

Salsa Preparation:

1. Prepare food processor.
2. Place onion and garlic in food processor and pulse several times until onion has a coarsely chopped, but not over-processed appearance.
3. Add cilantro, jalapeno, lime juice, tomatoes, and hot cayenne pepper.
4. Process until salsa is desired consistency but not mushy.
5. Add salt and pepper to taste.

BRAIN BOOSTERS
50 best brain foods: red bell pepper, black beans, avocado, tomatoes,
Brain healthy spices: garlic

A FRESH APPROACH: *If you prefer fresh salsa you can dice all the vegetables and simply blend them together. Instead of putting the vegetables in the food processor, allow them to blend together in the refrigerator for 30 minutes prior to serving so the flavors will "marry."*

Nutrition Per Serving, Whole Recipe

405 Calories	13 g Protein
48 g Carbohydrates	22 g Fat
10 g Saturated Fat	0 mg Cholesterol
888 mg Sodium	6 g Fiber

Nutrition Per Serving, Salsa

30 Calories	1 g Protein
7 g Carbohydrates	0 g Fat
0 g Saturated Fat	0 mg Cholesterol
570 mg Sodium	2 g Fiber

◆ **4 Servings** ◆ **296 Calories** ◆ **8 Brain Boosters**

DINNER

Ingredients:

2 chicken breasts

2 tablespoons refined coconut oil or olive oil

1 lime, juiced

1 tablespoon red wine vinegar

2 tablespoons cilantro, finely chopped

½ teaspoon paprika

1 teaspoon chili powder

½ teaspoon garlic powder

½ teaspoon onion powder

½ teaspoon Real Salt

Pepper, to taste

Pinch of cayenne pepper, to taste

Optional: 1 jalapeno pepper, seeded and finely chopped

Ingredients for Veggie Kabobs:

1 cup red, yellow, or green bell pepper (mixed), chunks

1 cup sweet red onion, chunks

1 cup mushroom caps

1 cup zucchini, chunks

1 cup yellow squash, chunks

Optional: 1 cup cherry tomatoes

Take note that the marinade for the chicken in this recipe can also be used to marinate the veggies, or you can use the Marinade Variation for the veggies. In any case, both versions of the marinade involve some of the same ingredients, so think ahead while you are chopping and juicing so you make enough for both the chicken and the veggies. It will save you time. Try doubling the marinade recipe.

Preparation for Chicken:

1. In a small mixing bowl, whisk together oil, lime juice, and vinegar. Add cilantro, paprika, chili powder, garlic powder, onion powder, cayenne pepper, and jalapeno (if using), salt, and pepper.
2. Place chicken breasts between pieces of waxed paper or plastic wrap. Pound lightly with meat mallet until chicken breasts are about ¼ inch thick.
3. Whisk marinade again before coating chicken breasts with mixture.
4. Place chicken breasts in baking dish and brush remaining marinade over breasts. Cover dish and refrigerate. If possible try to marinate for at least 2 hours so meat will be tender and flavorful. Marinate no less than 1 hour and no longer than 24 hours.
5. Heat grill to medium. Cover chicken while grilling.
6. Grill chicken for 8-10 minutes, turning once. Check one piece by cutting into the center. Center should not be pink.

Nutrition Per Serving, Whole Recipe

296 Calories	19 g Protein
14 g Carbohydrates	19 g Fat
3 g Saturated Fat	44 mg Cholesterol
926 mg Sodium	3 g Fiber

◆ **4 Servings** ◆ **296 Calories** ◆ **8 Brain Boosters**

Marinade Variation:

2 garlic cloves, minced

3 tablespoons olive oil

1 tablespoon red wine vinegar

2 lemons, juiced

1 teaspoon Real Salt

¼ teaspoon pepper

2 tablespoons fresh sage, chopped

Preparation for Veggies:

1. Whisk all ingredients together in a small mixing bowl. This recipe calls for olive oil because coconut oil will get hard in the refrigerator. The other option is to use coconut oil and not marinate the vegetables.
2. Put vegetables in the smallest bowl that they will easily fit in.
3. Pour marinade over vegetables and toss.
4. Cover and refrigerate for minimum of 2 hours, up to 8 hours. Toss veggies at least once during marinating time.
5. Remove from refrigerator and thread vegetables onto wooden skewers. Alternate vegetables by color for attractive kabobs.
6. Grill over medium heat for 8-10 minutes, turning occasionally. Cook a little less time for crispy veggies (healthier), or until slightly charred for more tender veggies.
7. Serve chicken and veggie kabobs together.

Optional: Consider serving with a side of guacamole.

Vegetarian Option: Serve the veggie kabobs without chicken and serve with a side of Nutted Couscous (page 93) or tofu.

BRAIN BOOSTERS
50 best brain foods: chicken, limes, bell peppers, tomatoes, olive oil, lemons
Brain healthy spices: garlic, sage

Nutrition Per Serving, Chicken Only	
154 Calories	16 g Protein
2 g Carbohydrates	9 g Fat
1 g Saturated Fat	44 mg Cholesterol
336 mg Sodium	0 g Fiber

Nutrition Per Serving, Veggies Only	
41 Calories	2 g Protein
9 g Carbohydrates	0 g Fat
0 g Saturated Fat	0 mg Cholesterol
7 mg Sodium	2 g Fiber

◆ **4 Servings** ◆ **312 Calories** ◆ **5 Brain Boosters**

Ingredients:

2 8-ounce sushi-grade ahi fillets
(I buy them from a source that
gets them fresh on a daily basis.)
1-2 tablespoons refined coconut
oil or ghee, for searing

Guacamole Ingredients:

1 ripe avocado, pitted and diced
2 tomatillos, finely chopped
2 teaspoons shallot clove,
minced
1 tablespoon fresh lime juice
½ teaspoon garlic salt
½ teaspoon pepper

Marinade Ingredients:

2 tablespoons cilantro, chopped
2 teaspoons fresh ginger, grated
1 shallot clove, minced
1 tablespoon fresh lime juice
2 tablespoons soy sauce
½ teaspoon Real Salt
¼ teaspoon black pepper
2 tablespoons refined coconut
oil

Preparation:

1. In a mixing bowl, mash avocado with a fork and mix in diced tomatillos. Stir in shallot, lime juice, salt, and pepper. Set aside until fish is finished.

2. Sprinkle tuna fillets with salt and pepper on both sides and set aside.

3. In a mixing bowl, combine cilantro, ginger, shallot, lime juice, soy sauce, honey, salt, pepper, and 2 tablespoons coconut oil.

4. Heat a large skillet over moderately high heat. Add 1-2 tablespoons of oil or ghee to heated skillet.

5. Place fillets in heated skillet for 1 minute on each side. Turn fillets to ensure that sides have been seared as well.

6. Pour cilantro marinade mix into the pan and coat the fish on both sides. Do not overcook.

7. Remove from pan. Either cut fillets in half or into thin slices and fan out on plates. Drizzle remaining marinade from pan onto the fish.

8. Top with guacamole and serve.

BRAIN BOOSTERS
50 best brain foods: ahi tuna, avocado, limes,
Brain healthy spices: garlic, ginger

Nutrition Per Serving, Whole Recipe	
312 Calories	30 g Protein
10 g Carbohydrates	18 g Fat
11 g Saturated Fat	52 mg Cholesterol
880 mg Sodium	3 g Fiber

Nutrition Per Serving, Guacamole Alone	
80 Calories	1 g Protein
5 g Carbohydrates	7 g Fat
1 g Saturated Fat	0 mg Cholesterol
249 mg Sodium	3 g Fiber

DINNER

♦ **10 Servings** ♦ **126 Calories** ♦ **7 Brain Boosters**

Ingredients:

1½ pounds lean ground turkey (organic, free range)
¾ cup old-fashioned oats, uncooked (do not use instant oats)
1 cup onion, chopped
½ teaspoon black pepper
1 teaspoon Real Salt
1 tablespoon fresh basil leaves, chopped
1 tablespoon fresh oregano, chopped
3 garlic cloves, minced
2 eggs or Egg Beaters (equivalent of 2 eggs)
½ cup tomato basil pasta sauce

Optional: For a southwestern flare, omit basil, oregano, and pasta sauce. Instead, use sage, 1 package of organic vegetable soup mix, and ½ cup of salsa.

Preparation:

1. Preheat oven to 350 degrees F.
2. In large mixing bowl, combine turkey, oats, onion, salt, pepper, basil, oregano, garlic, eggs, and ¾ cup of the pasta sauce. Mix well. If you prefer, you can place onion, basil, oregano, and garlic in food processor to mix.
3. Press mixture into a 9 X 5 inch bread loaf pan.
4. Spread remaining pasta sauce over the top. This should be a thin coat to prevent the loaf from drying during baking.
5. Bake for approximately 60 minutes or until internal temperature is 160 degrees F.

BRAIN BOOSTERS
50 best brain foods: turkey, oats, eggs, tomatoes (in the pasta sauce)
Brain healthy spices: basil, oregano, garlic

QUICK-BAKING HINTS: *If you wish to cut the baking time, try pressing the mixture into a larger cake pan instead. This will ensure that the loaf cooks through more evenly and quickly. Otherwise, try putting a hole in the center of the loaf in the bread pan.*

Nutrition Per Serving

126 Calories	18 g Protein
7 g Carbohydrates	3 g Fat
1 g Saturated Fat	51 mg Cholesterol
346 mg Sodium	1 g Fiber

♦ **4 Servings** ♦ **199 Calories** ♦ **8 Brain Boosters**

Ingredients:

1 8-ounce package of tempeh or seitan, both meat substitutions

Optional: Use shrimp for non-vegetarians

2 cups brown rice, cooked

1 tablespoon refined coconut oil or 3-4 tablespoons vegetable broth, for sautéing

½ yellow onion, thinly sliced

¼ cup carrot, shredded

1 garlic clove, minced

1 tablespoon fresh thyme, finely chopped

1 bunch asparagus, cut into 1-inch pieces (discard tough ends)

1 cup cabbage, thinly sliced

½ cup red bell pepper, thinly sliced

1 handful snow peas

1 teaspoon ginger, finely grated

1 teaspoon fennel seeds

1 teaspoon curry powder

2 tablespoons low-sodium soy sauce

Optional: 2 teaspoons cornstarch (to make a thicker sauce and prevent pooling of liquid from vegetables)

When I make this dish at home, I don't add the tempeh, seitan, or shrimp. I simply add some slivered almonds to the stir-fry. Between the fresh, *lightly* cooked vegetables and the nuts there is plenty of protein for most people. You can always add a cup of quinoa and a big salad to dramatically increase your protein intake.

Preparation for Veggies:

1. Prepare brown rice according to directions while cooking stir-fry.
2. If using tempeh, steam tempeh with ginger and fennel seeds for 20 minutes in a steamer basket. Be sure not to allow water to bathe tempeh. Remove from steamer and mix with soy sauce and garlic. Marinate for 1 hour.
3. Heat wok or large skillet over medium-high heat. Add coconut oil and coat surface of pan.
4. Add onion and sauté for 1 minute, then add carrot and sauté for another minute.
5. Add garlic, thyme, asparagus, cabbage, bell pepper, and snow peas. Cook until asparagus are tender but not overcooked, about 3 minutes.
6. Add tempeh and soy marinade to skillet.
7. Dissolve cornstarch in ¼ cup water, add to skillet, and stir in well. Bring to a boil for 1 minute. Remove from heat.
8. Add ½ - 1 cup steamed rice to each plate and serve stir-fry over the top.

BRAIN BOOSTERS
50 best brain foods: carrots, asparagus, red bell pepper, almonds
Brain healthy spices: garlic, thyme, ginger, curry

Nutrition Per Serving	
199 Calories	11 g Protein
26 g Carbohydrates	7 g Fat
3 g Saturated Fat	0 mg Cholesterol
213 mg Sodium	4 g Fiber

COCONUT CURRY NOODLES

◆ **6 Servings** ◆ **272 Calories** ◆ **8 Brain Boosters**

Ingredients:

1 large spaghetti squash
1 bunch scallions, cut in 2-inch pieces on an angle
1 carrot, thinly sliced
1 cup broccoli florets
½ pound asparagus, cut in 2-inch diagonals
1 red bell pepper, thinly sliced
1 yellow squash, sliced
4 tiny bok choy, leaves separated
½ pound snow peas

Sauce Ingredients:

2-inch piece of ginger root, peeled and grated
2 garlic cloves
1 tablespoon organic soy sauce
2 tablespoons sesame oil
2 tablespoons flaxseed oil
1 teaspoon curry paste
1 teaspoon thyme
¼ teaspoon garlic salt
1 cup coconut milk, unsweetened
1 tablespoon corn starch dissolved in ¼ cup water

Optional: You may add ½ teaspoon

Preparation:

1. Preheat oven to 375 degrees F.
2. Cut spaghetti squash in half. Clean out seeds. Fill baking dish ¼ full of water. Place squash face down on a baking dish and place in oven for about 45 minutes.
3. Steam vegetables in order. Boil small amount of water in a large pot. Place steamer basket in water so that water does not go over basket. You don't want the water to bathe the vegetables as they are being steamed. After water boils, reduce to simmer.
4. Place scallions in bottom of basket. Next place carrots, then broccoli, then asparagus, then red bell pepper, then squash, then bok choy, then snow peas.
5. Steam for about 3-4 minutes. I prefer my vegetables on the crunchy side. It is much healthier, and tastier.
6. Turn off heat and set aside.

Sauce Preparation:

1. Blend ginger root, garlic, and soy sauce in food processor until smooth.
2. Add sesame and flax oils, curry paste, thyme, garlic salt, coconut milk, and red pepper flakes. Pulse several times.
3. Heat sauce in small pot over medium heat. Add cornstarch and water mixture. Bring to a boil then remove from heat until spaghetti squash and vegetables are finished cooking.
4. Place spaghetti squash in a large serving dish with vegetable arranged on top.
5. Drizzle sauce over the top and serve remaining sauce on the side.
6. Serve hot.

BRAIN BOOSTERS
50 best brain foods: carrots, broccoli, asparagus, red bell pepper
Brain healthy spices: ginger, garlic, curry, thyme

Nutrition Per Serving, Whole Recipe

272 Calories   5 g Protein
20 g Carbohydrates   22 g Fat
11 g Saturated Fat   0 mg Cholesterol
380 mg Sodium   6 g Fiber

Nutrition Per Serving, Sauce Alone

178 Calories   1 g Protein
3 g Carbohydrates   19 g Fat
10 g Saturated Fat   0 mg Cholesterol
332 mg Sodium   1 g Fiber

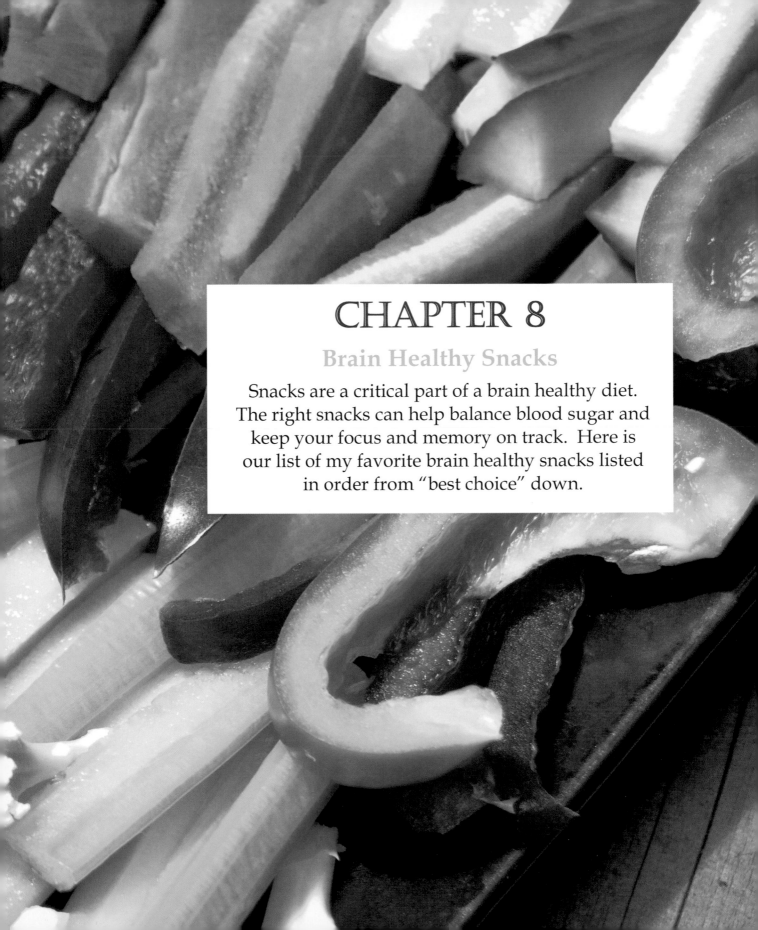

CHAPTER 8

Brain Healthy Snacks

Snacks are a critical part of a brain healthy diet.
The right snacks can help balance blood sugar and
keep your focus and memory on track. Here is
our list of my favorite brain healthy snacks listed
in order from "best choice" down.

One of the first things you should always do before grabbing a snack is drink a large glass of water. You may be very surprised at how much 16 ounces of water with "greens" added will decrease your appetite for unhealthy or unnecessary snacks. Often when you believe you are hungry, your body is actually dehydrated. Hydrating your system and giving it the nutrients it needs with "greens" will often minimize unwanted cravings.

1. Cut mixed vegetables (such as bell peppers, celery, cucumbers, broccoli, and cauliflower). If you need more flavor or sustenance, try dipping veggies in hummus, baba ghanoush, guacamole, or salsa. Remember that although these dips are very healthy, they are calorie dense (except salsa), so pay attention to how much you are eating.

2. Soaked raw almonds. Presoak almonds in water so they are ready to go. They make a fantastic snack and are very satisfying. Soaking them serves several purposes. It starts the sprouting process, loads the almonds with water making them more filling and water dense (which is healthier), and makes them tastier and easier to eat for most people. Note: roasted almonds don't count!

3. Fresh guacamole on gluten-free or sprouted grain toast. I make a quick and simplified version of guacamole when I'm in a hurry. I simply mash half an avocado in a bowl and add a few drops of lemon juice and a tiny bit of garlic salt. This is a very filling and satisfying snack.

4. Celery with 2 tablespoons of organic, raw almond butter.

5. A banana, apple, or other low-glycemic fruit.

6. Sliced apple dipped in raw almond butter.

7. ½ cup fresh or frozen organic blueberries with ¼ cup coconut milk or rice yogurt.

8. Steamed edamame with a pinch of Real Salt.

9. Meal-replacement protein bars. These are not my first choice, but they are good in a pinch. Sometimes I carry them when I'm traveling and unable to plan meals as effectively as usual. Be sure to read labels when choosing, as many labels can be misleading. Most of these bars are loaded with sugar. Find bars that are sweetened with unrefined sweeteners and are low in overall sugar or sweetened with malitol, sorbitol, or erythritol. Also, I prefer bars that use protein sources from soy or rice as opposed to milk proteins.

10. Rice crackers or baked sweet potato chips with fresh salsa. Pay attention to calories and fat when choosing this snack.

11. Protein shake (soy or rice protein) with fresh or frozen fruit.

12. One-half of a baked sweet potato with 1 teaspoon Earth Balance buttery spread.

13. Popcorn with Earth Balance sauce. To make buttery sauce, melt 1 tablespoon Earth Balance, 1 teaspoon Spike Seasoning or Cayenne pepper, and Real Salt. Slowly drizzle sauce over popcorn while mixing.

14. Small can of tuna mixed with 2 teaspoons Veganaise and served on celery or bell peppers.

15. For non-vegetarians, sliced turkey breast (not packaged lunch meat that contains nitrates) and cantaloupe.

16. Deviled eggs with hummus. Slice the eggs, discard the yolks, fill with 1 tablespoon hummus, and add paprika to taste.

17. Turkey and apple slices with a macadamia nut or 3 almonds.

CHAPTER 9

Deceivingly Light & Healthy Desserts

We love dessert at our house. It is part of our daily lives.
Check out these recipes to make dessert choices work for
you rather than hurt you.

DESSERT

♦ **2 Servings** ♦ **97 Calories** ♦ **2 Brain Boosters** ♦ **Gluten-Free**

Ingredients:

16 ounces frozen blueberries
8 ounces coconut yogurt
10 drops plain or vanilla-
flavored stevia (Sweet Leaf is
my favorite brand)

Preparation:

1. Mix all ingredients in a large bowl.
2. Dish into dessert bowls and serve cold.

BRAIN BOOSTERS
50 best brain foods: blueberries, yogurt

Nutrition Per Serving

97 Calories	1 g Protein
16 g Carbohydrates	4 g Fat
3 g Saturated Fat	0 mg Cholesterol
5 mg Sodium	3 g Fiber

◆ **2 Servings** ◆ **60 Calories** ◆ **3 Brain Boosters**

Ingredients:

20-24 ounces plain almond milk
(preferably unsweetened)
2 green chai tea bags (I like Stash brand)
10 drops vanilla or cinnamon-flavored stevia (Sweet Leaf brand is my favorite)

This is my all-time favorite when I have a craving for something sweet and warm. It is totally satisfying and filling without the fat, sugar, and calories of a traditional chai tea latte… and I get my daily green tea at the same time.

Preparation:

1. Heat almond milk in medium sauce pan over medium heat until milk begins to boil. Turn off heat immediately or milk will boil over.
2. Pour milk into a teapot to keep warm while steeping or divide evenly between 2 cups.
3. Add tea bags to each cup and let steep for minutes.
4. Add 5 drops of stevia to each cup (or to taste).
5. Serve hot.

BRAIN BOOSTERS

50 best brain foods: almond milk, green tea
Brain healthy spices: cinnamon

Nutrition Per Serving

60 Calories	2 g Protein
3 g Carbohydrates	5 g Fat
0 g Saturated Fat	0 mg Cholesterol
270 mg Sodium	2 g Fiber

BANANA ICE DREAM SUNDAY

♦ **4 Servings** ♦ **269 Calories** ♦ **5 Brain Boosters**

DESSERT

Ingredients:

6 frozen bananas (slice bananas and place in Ziploc bag over night with 1 teaspoon fresh lemon juice to prevent browning)

2 dates, soaked (need to soak for at least 20 minutes) and cut into quarters

¼ cup almonds, soaked (need to soak almonds in refrigerator for at least 2 hours, up to 24 hours)

Splash of water or unsweetened almond milk, for blending

1 scoop Amazing Greens chocolate-flavored green mix

1 cup fresh blueberries, strawberries, or any other fresh fruit

Optional: 1 scoop soy or whey Protein

Optional: 1-2 packets stevia to taste

Optional: 3 tablespoons shaved coconut

Preparation:

1. Place frozen banana slices in blender or food processor with soaked dates and soaked almonds. Turn on blender. Add just enough liquid to allow blending. Be sure to keep consistency thick.
2. After about 30-60 seconds, add Amazing Greens, stevia, and protein powder (if desired). Blend for an additional 10-30 seconds. Do not over-blend protein!
3. Scoop into martini glasses or dessert bowls and top with fresh blueberries, other fruit, or shaved coconut.

BRAIN BOOSTERS
50 best brain foods: bananas, almonds, almond milk, blueberries, strawberries

FOR CHOCOLATE LOVERS ONLY: *A chocolaty syrup can be made by blending a couple soaked dates with a couple tablespoons of carob powder with a splash of water or almond milk. This is not my first choice because the natural sugar in the carob powder over-acidifies the human body's system. Even natural sugar is still sugar! But if you are playing "hostess with the mostess" for an evening, this is a far better choice than Triple Chocolate Chunk or Jamocha Devil Almond Fudge.*

Nutrition Per Serving

269 Calories	6 g Protein
93 g Carbohydrates	6 g Fat
0 g Saturated Fat	0 mg Cholesterol
13 mg Sodium	15 g Fiber

◆ **2 Servings** ◆ **80 Calories** ◆ **4 Brain Boosters**

Ingredients:

1 lemon, zest and juice
½ cup fresh strawberries, sliced
½ cup fresh raspberries
1 cup fresh blueberries
Vanilla-flavored stevia (5-10 drops, to taste)

* Optional: shaved coconut for topping

Preparation:

1. Add lemon juice, zest, and fruit to blender. Blend for 30-60 seconds.
2. Add stevia a couple drops at a time. Do not over-sweeten or it will taste bitter.
3. Blend until smooth.
4. Serve immediately.

Preparation for Ice Cream Maker:

1. Add lemon juice, zest, and fruit to a blender and purée.
2. Pour fruit mixture through metal strainer. Discard pulp and seeds.
3. Add stevia a couple drops at a time and mix. Do not over-sweeten or it will taste bitter.
4. Follow instructions on ice cream maker to freeze fruit mixture. This usually takes several hours.

BRAIN BOOSTERS

50 best brain foods: lemons, strawberries, raspberries, blueberries

NO ICE CREAM MAKER? NO PROBLEM! *For a quick and simple version not using an ice cream maker, follow the same instructions above, but use frozen fruit and do not strain mixture. Simply blend all ingredients and serve immediately.*

Nutrition Per Serving	
80 Calories	2 g Protein
23 g Carbohydrates	0 g Fat
0 g Saturated Fat	0 mg Cholesterol
3 mg Sodium	6 g Fiber

CHOCOLATE-COVERED STRAWBERRY MOUSSE

DESSERT

♦ **4 Servings** ♦ **352 Calories** ♦ **3 Brain Boosters**

Ingredients:

7 ounces soft tofu (about ½ of
1 14-ounce package)
¼ cup almond milk
1 tablespoon carob powder
(start with 1 tablespoon and
add as desired, but note that
carob powder will taste bitter
if you add too much)
¾ cup raw almond butter
1 cup fresh strawberries,
sliced
10-12 drops stevia liquid
sweetener or 1-2 tablespoons
agave nectar
Nondairy whipped cream
topping

*Optional: carob chips or carob
shavings*

*Optional: shaved coconut for
topping*

Preparation:

1. Place ¼ cup of sliced strawberries in the bottom of 4 dessert dishes or martini glasses.
2. Put tofu, almond milk, carob powder, almond butter, and agave or stevia into blender. Blend until smooth and creamy.
3. Pour mousse on top of strawberry slices. Chill for at least one hour.
4. Top each dessert with a small amount of nondairy whipped cream. Place one strawberry on top.

BRAIN BOOSTERS
50 best brain foods: tofu, almond milk

Nutrition Per Serving

352 Calories   11 g Protein
15 g Carbohydrates   30 g Fat
3 g Saturated Fat   0 mg Cholesterol
22 mg Sodium   2 g Fiber

DESSERT

◆ **2 Servings** ◆ **425 Calories** ◆ **3 Brain Boosters**

Ingredients:

2 bananas (frozen if desired)

¼ cup blueberries

1 tablespoon golden raisins

½ cup chocolate almond milk, unsweetened

½ cup chocolate soy or coconut milk ice cream

1 scoop whey protein

1 scoop Green Vibrance (powdered greens)

5 drops chocolate raspberry stevia

Ice, as desired

This still has some refined sugar from the sorbet or soy ice cream and should not be a regular treat, but it is better than a traditional milkshake. When my daughter is not feeling well and will not eat, I give this to her as an energy booster and a way to ensure she is getting enough protein.

Preparation:

1. Put banana, blueberries, raisins, almond milk, and "ice cream" in blender. Blend 30-60 seconds or until smooth. Add ice as necessary and blend for 30-60 seconds for thick milkshake consistency.
2. Add protein powder, Green Vibrance, and stevia. Blend no more than 10 seconds.
3. Serve immediately.

BRAIN BOOSTERS
50 best brain foods: bananas, almond milk, blueberries

Nutrition Per Serving

425 Calories	17 g Protein
77 g Carbohydrates	17 g Fat
14 g Saturated Fat	33 mg Cholesterol
224 mg Sodium	4 g Fiber

♦ **2 Servings** ♦ **292 Calories** ♦ **2 Brain Boosters**

Ingredients:

2-3 cups coconut milk

1½ cups coconut milk yogurt, plain or vanilla flavor

3 cups frozen strawberries

1 tablespoon raw wheat germ

2 tablespoons shaved coconut flakes

Optional: 10 drops vanilla-flavored stevia

Preparation:

1. Add milk, yogurt, strawberries, wheat germ, coconut flakes, and stevia to a blender. Blend for 30-60 seconds or until smooth and creamy.
2. Pour into tall glasses and top with a little shaved coconut.
3. Serve cold.

BRAIN BOOSTERS

50 best brain foods: yogurt, strawberries

Nutrition Per Serving

292 Calories	4 g Protein
51 g Carbohydrates	9 g Fat
6 g Saturated Fat	0 mg Cholesterol
165 mg Sodium	11 g Fiber

CHOCOLATE NUT ICE DREAM BARS

◆ **2 Servings** ◆ **114 Calories** ◆ **3 Brain Boosters**

DESSERT

Ingredients:

4 frozen bananas

2 tablespoons raw almond butter

1 teaspoon carob powder

¼ cup coconut milk yogurt, plain flavor

¼ cup chocolate almond milk, unsweetened

10 drops liquid stevia (English toffee or chocolate are excellent. I prefer Sweet Leaf brand.)

*Optional: 1 handful vegan carob chips

Advance Preparation

1. Peel and cut bananas into thirds, place in a Ziploc bag, and freeze for several hours.

Preparation:

1. Put frozen banana pieces in a blender with almond butter, carob powder, yogurt, almond milk, and stevia. Blend on highest level or "Ice Cream" setting until smooth and creamy.
2. Pour into popsicle trays, place sticks in the center, and freeze for several hours for delicious-tasting Ice Dream Bars.
3. Serve frozen.

BRAIN BOOSTERS

50 best brain foods: bananas, yogurt, almond milk

Nutrition Per Serving

114 Calories	3 g Protein
37 g Carbohydrates	4 g Fat
0 g Saturated Fat	0 mg Cholesterol
9 mg Sodium	5 g Fiber

♦ **2 Servings** ♦ **292 Calories** ♦ **2 Brain Boosters**

Ingredients:

¼ cup frozen or thawed blueberries (preferably wild and organic)

1 tablespoon raw almond butter

Optional: Drizzle with a few drops of agave nectar.

Preparation:

1. Let the blueberries thaw for 30 minutes and then mash them with a fork in a bowl.
2. Mix them with the almond butter. If the berries are not thawed and you mash them while frozen, it will then taste more like an ice-cream.

BRAIN BOOSTERS
50 best brain foods: blueberries, almonds

Variations:

- Use ⅛ cup blueberries and ⅛ cup raspberries or blackberries. If you want it very tangy, use frozen cranberries but they take longer to thaw and smash.

- If you can afford the carbs, you may add half a mashed banana , it will make it very creamy and sweet.

- If you want to add some protein, mix a tablespoon of rice protein powder (or whey) with a tablespoon of water. This has a similar taste and texture to cream (without the fat). It gives the impression that cream was added.

- Almond butter fat is highly monounsaturated and full of antioxidants, unlike cream which is all saturated fat.

Nutrition Per Serving

292 Calories	4 g Protein
51 g Carbohydrates	9 g Fat
6 g Saturated Fat	0 mg Cholesterol
165 mg Sodium	11 g Fiber

DESSERT

◆ **12 Servings** ◆ **114 Calories** ◆ **4 Brain Boosters** ◆ **Gluten-Free**

Pie Crust Ingredients:

1 cup almond flour (Bob's Red
    Mill brand has no almond skins
    and has a very smooth flavor)

½ cup rice or whey protein (This
    is a substitute for cream in
    conventional recipes)

2 tablespoons unsweetened
    coconut, medium or finely
    shredded (or coconut flour)

2-4 tablespoons of xylitol or
    erythritol sweetener (or
    substitute part of it with agave
    or maple syrup)

4 tablespoons refined coconut oil

1 teaspoon vanilla

½ teaspoon cinnamon

*Optional: 1 egg (this will make it
    less flaky)*

Optional: ½ teaspoon Real Sea Salt

Preparation:

1. Preheat oven to 325 degrees F.
2. Mix all dry ingredients together with a whisk in a bowl.
3. Melt the coconut oil or butter and pour it in the dry mix, blending well with the fork.
4. Chill this mix for 15 minutes in the refrigerator.
5. If using egg, beat separately and mix it in the chilled mix.
6. Dust the pie pan with rice flour or corn starch. It is best to use a Pyrex pie dish or a non-toxic enameled pie pan instead of the common aluminum pie pans.
7. Scoop the mix from the mixing bowl and press it evenly into the pie pan with a spoon. You will have some pie crust mix leftover, which you can use to bake on the side like a cookie (this is your tester to see when it is done).
8. Bake for approximately 10-12 minutes and watch it so it does not brown too much.
9. Remove from oven and cool for 15 minutes at room temperature, then refrigerate crust for 15 minutes to chill.

Nutrition Per Serving, Pie Crust	
114 Calories	3 g Protein
37 g Carbohydrates	4 g Fat
0 g Saturated Fat	0 mg Cholesterol
9 mg Sodium	5 g Fiber

◆ **12 Servings** ◆ **292 Calories** ◆ **4 Brain Boosters**

Pumpkin Filling Ingredients:

1 can organic pumpkin, unsweetened (approximately 3½ cups)

1 cup apple sauce, unsweetened

1 cup rice or whey protein and 1 cup water (this is a substitute for cream)

½ cup almond flour

4-6 teaspoons of stevia or 4-6 tablespoons of xylitol or erythritol sweetener (or substitute part of it with agave or maple syrup)

2 packets Knox gelatin with 1 cup of water or may substitute with vegetarian gum (xanthan gum or guar gum)

Pumpkin Filling Preparation:

1. Mix all ingredients, except gelatin, with a whisk in a pan and heat it slowly to make sure the ingredients melt and blend together.
2. Melt the contents of 2 Knox gelatin packets in a pan with 1 cup of water for a few minutes until the liquid is clear and smooth.
3. Pour the melted liquid gelatin in the pie mix and blend with a whisk. Then pour this mix into a blender to make sure it is very smooth.
4. Pour the mix into the chilled pie crust and let is chill in the refrigerator for at least 4-6 hours.
5. May serve with non-dairy or regular whip cream.

BRAIN BOOSTERS
50 best brain foods: almonds (in the almond flour), water, egg
Brain healthy spices: cinnamon

Nutrition Per Serving, Pumpkin Filling

292 Calories	4 g Protein
51 g Carbohydrates	9 g Fat
6 g Saturated Fat	0 mg Cholesterol
165 mg Sodium	11 g Fiber

CHAPTER 10
Creating Brain Healthy Parties

Being part of a large Lebanese family does not make eating healthy at family gatherings and parties a simple task unless we really set our minds to it. If you know anything about Middle Eastern cultures, you know that food is the central theme around which families and friends gather and bond. Not only is cooking and sharing food something we do to show our appreciation and love for those we care about, but it is often considered an insult or personal rejection to turn down the food that has taken hours to prepare.

It has traditionally been acceptable to be a little "thick in the middle," and actually considered less attractive to be too thin.   When visiting my aunt in Pennsylvania, the first thing I usually hear upon arriving is, "Oh my! We need to put some weight on you! I have been cooking all weekend. You need to eat." She would stand over me and literally try to put food in my mouth. It was her way of showing love.

If we are going to change the health of our society, we need to change our association to food. We don't need to eliminate our love of gathering, bonding, or even the desire to have food as a central theme. If we put as much energy into creating "brain healthy" choices at our parties and gatherings the outcome would be astounding.

The key is to change your focus and motivation. Instead of thinking about how much you want to impress everyone with your gourmet skills, get clear on what you are really doing and what the real motivation is, or at least could or should be. Be clear that traditional party food and most gourmet foods are filled with fat, salt, sugar, and many other unhealthy ingredients.   Start with empowering questions that help to define your goal.

•*How can I create an outstanding party that will leave my guests even healthier and more energetic?*

•*How can I set an example that being healthy and fit is easy and fun?*

Creating brain healthy parties is not very difficult and will eliminate at least some of the pressure and work traditionally associated with the food portion of party planning. I recently had a surprise birthday party for my husband. I invited more than 100 guests. Knowing that most of the guests would be very health conscious, I knew that I would have to provide at least some of the food myself. However, I also had much of the food catered simply because of the number of people attending. An interesting thing happened.

We brought the food out in stages, starting with large platters of fresh fruit and vegetables, accompanied by fresh salsa, guacamole, hummus, baba ghanoush, and non-dairy yogurt dip. There were also bowls of raw nuts sitting around. Along with this course was tabouleh and a cucumber mint salad. The next round of food came about 45 minutes later and included grilled vegetables, artichokes, grilled shrimp, seared ahi, and a couple other things. The least healthy of the food (because of the sauce), was grilled fish, chicken, and pork. I found it fascinating that the meat was all but untouched. Hardly anyone ate it. The least healthy thing that I served at the party was birthday cake (come on, even I'm not a total party pooper!). Again, it was virtually untouched.

As I cleaned up the aftermath of the party, I couldn't help but analyze the remains. The food that I had spent the most money for remained, while the fruit, vegetables, salads, and healthier fare had been devoured. One reason may have been because of an oversight on my part not having the sauces served on the side. Or it could have been that the crowd was a fairly health-conscious crowd.

However, I really believe it had more to do with the fact that the guests were offered so many healthy choices to fill up on *first!* By the time the heavier meats and sauces were brought out the guests had already had time to nibble and graze on fresh, healthy food arranged on beautiful platters.

I learned two very important lessons from this experience.

Lesson One: It doesn't matter how exclusive the guest list is, your guests will appreciate fresh, healthy food that has been beautifully presented. You don't need to spend hundreds or even thousands of dollars on food that will make your guests fat and tired. If you are going to spend the money, spend it on something healthy.

Lesson Two: Bringing food out in courses is a *really* good idea. Think about it. No matter how beautifully you decorate your house, where do people congregate? *The kitchen!* We have established that people often gather with food being the central theme. So let them! Bring the food out slowly, in courses. Let your guests graze and nibble slowly. Allow them to fill up on healthy choices prior to serving the main course. You can bet that they will eat smaller portions, which is much healthier.

Even if you are planning a more traditional, sit-down dinner, plan some time in advance for people to visit and munch on healthy appetizers. You don't have to serve traditional, fat-filled dishes. Your main courses can be healthy, creative, and unique.

1. Always serve raw fruits and vegetables first, along with fresh salsa, guacamole, hummus, and baba ghanoush.

2. Serve whole-grain bread or pita bread as an alternative to chips. Baked chips can also be an alternative. Fried chips have acrilomide (a known carcinogen).

3. Next bring out some refreshing salads such as Barley Tabouleh, a lighter version of traditional tabouleh (page 46), Cool Cucumber Mint Salad (page 51), or Quinoa Salad (page 44).

4. If you are doing the cooking yourself: Stick to dishes that can be cooked in large portions without much extra effort. Some suggestions: Try grilled vegetables with a light vinaigrette sauce, grilled fish, or kabobs. If you are serving chicken, fish, or kabobs of any kind, preparation can be done well in advance so that you only need to spend a few minutes grilling.

5. If you are planning to use a caterer: Make sure you understand what the ingredients are in the sauces they are serving. Do not trust them if they tell you they are "light" and "everyone likes them." Have them serve all sauces on the side. If you are serving food in the fashion mentioned above, you will likely not need as much food as you think you will. I can easily order main courses for half the number of guests. Most of the guests do not take as large a portion as is normally served. I still usually end up with lots of excess food.

6. End with something fresh and light for dessert. Your guests won't miss the flourless chocolate cake. A favorite at our parties is the Revitalizing Fruit Salad (page 47) with mint dressing. If you really want to have something decadent, try putting out a bowl of "healthy" chocolates. There are a couple brands of dark chocolate that are sweetened with fruit juice or acai berries. One brand has an ORAC value of over 11,000 and has very little caffeine.

7. Know your guest list well. Be aware of any special dietary needs of guests. Know if there is a guest who is diabetic or if you will be having guests who are vegan (vegans do not consume any animal products, including eggs, dairy, or honey). Vegan diets are becoming increasingly popular. It is a good idea to provide a menu healthy enough to feed either of these dietary needs. Have at least a couple of tasty options available.

8. Do not be afraid to ask for help from close friends and family. One of the greatest things about marrying into my new family is the abundance of love and help at my fingertips at any given time. While it was difficult for me to ask for help initially, I found that when I did it created a stronger sense of family… for me! My new family gladly helped, and they began to bond with me. As I said, Middle Eastern families love to gather around food. It's likely that you will find some of the people in your own circles who feel the same. It is a party after all.

Hosting a party with brain healthy fare is easy. The tasty finger foods listed here include many of the 50 Best Brain Foods and Brain Healthy Spices—you'll find these brain-enhancing foods and spices in **bold**. Packed with potent antioxidants and nutrients, these party foods will boost brain function for an unforgettable soirée.

Holiday Spiced Green Tea

Mix **green tea** leaves with chopped and dried **orange** peel, chopped and dried **ginger** root, and **cinnamon**. Add **unsweetened almond milk** for a healthy version of a chai tea. Consider cinnamon-flavored stevia as a sweetener if desired.

Spa Water
Serve sparkling or flat **water** with **lemon** or **lime** wedges. Lemon-flavored stevia makes this taste like lemonade… even children love it.

Raw Veggies Tray
Broccoli florets
Red, yellow, orange, and green bell peppers
Cherry **tomatoes**
Carrots

Fruit Bowl
Fill a bowl with **cherries**

Cheese Tray
Pair **low-fat cheese** with fruit like **apples**

Hummus
Made from **garbanzo beans, lemon** juice, tahini, **olive oil**, and **garlic**

Guacamole
Mix **avocado** with onions, **tomatoes**, serrano chiles, and **lime** or **lemon** juice

Salsa
Combine **tomatoes**, onions, cilantro, jalapeno peppers, **lime, garlic** powder, cumin (found in **curry**)

Black Bean Dip
Purée low-salt or no-salt canned **black beans**, red onion, **orange** or **lime** juice, cilantro, **olive oil, garlic**, and cumin (found in **curry**) in a blender

PARTIES

Mixed Nuts
Walnuts, almonds, cashews, and peanuts
(preferrably raw — roasting nuts eliminates most of the nutritional value and leaves you with the bad fat and salt)

Bruschetta
Use **whole wheat** bread instead of white bread and top with heirloom **tomatoes**, a little **olive oil**, and lots of fresh **basil**

Smoked Wild Salmon
Serve smoked **wild salmon** with **lemon**, capers, and dill on **whole wheat** toast points

Chicken Skewers
Grill **chicken breasts** marinated in **plain coconut milk yogurt**, **curry**, fresh **ginger**, and **garlic**

Shrimp Kebabs
Marinate **shrimp** in **olive oil**, **garlic**, and **lemon**

Shrimp Cocktail
Serve jumbo **shrimp** with homemade cocktail sauce made with salsa, horseradish, and **lemon** juice

Sushi
Wrap sushi-grade **wild salmon** or **tuna**, **avocado**, cucumber, and **asparagus** in just a little brown rice then wrap with seaweed

Edamame
Cooked **soybeans** go great with sushi

Yogurt Parfait
Top **plain Greek yogurt** (or non-dairy coconut milk yogurt with live cultures) with **blueberries**, **strawberries**, and **raspberries**, then sprinkle with chopped **almonds** for a tasty dessert

ACKNOWLEDGEMENTS

It is an honor to write this cookbook in cooperation with my husband Daniel whose inspiration and continued support have helped me and our family to change our brains and lives to be happier, healthier, and more fulfilled. Working with Daniel has added to the respect I have for him as a doctor, partner, and friend. Having a partner who supports me in pursuing my passions and dreams is a priceless treasure.

Special thanks to Kamila for her undying patience in helping to test many of these recipes repeatedly through this process. Kamila is a culinary master. With our demanding schedules, this process would have been delayed much longer without the expert assistance of Kamila in testing recipes on a daily basis.

My deep appreciation goes to Frances Sharpe and Catherine Miller for their research assistance. Organization of information is a large part of this project. Catherine and Frances have been invaluable.

Finally, I would like to give special thanks to our photographer "Vince Weathermon" for his artistry in illustrating these creations so beautifully. He manages to create a canvas that captures the visual essence of each dish.

Tana K. Amen, BSN

Tana Amen graduated from Loma Linda University with a Bachelor's of Science Degree in Nursing and has worked as a Trauma/Neurosurgical ICU nurse.

Tana is a health enthusiast and has been focused on fitness for over two decades. She also worked with some of the sickest patients in the hospital and saw the effects of poor lifestyle choices and the intense need for special nutrition when patients were healing from brain injuries and other traumas.

In spite of her medical and fitness background, Tana was repeatedly surprised when her own health failed her throughout the years. She was diagnosed with thyroid cancer at the age of 25. How could someone who lived a consciously healthy lifestyle be diagnosed with cancer and the numerous other health issues that presented themselves over the years? That's when she began to further her education about nutrition and the role it plays on overall health.

Tana began to realize that "health" and "fitness" are not synonymous. Furthermore, she came to the conclusion that many of the basic nutrition principles she had learned in her youth were outdated and not enough to optimize *wellness* in a person's life. There is a major difference between sustenance and optimal nutrition for a *high-energy, passionately healthy lifestyle!*

Tana is the nutrition and fitness leader of the Amen household. She practices martial arts regularly, has a black belt in Tae Kwon Do, and enjoys a variety of other physical activities. Keeping her family focused on fitness and *health* is a primary value for Tana.

Daniel G. Amen, MD

Daniel G. Amen, MD, is a physician, child and adult psychiatrist, brain-imaging specialist, and *New York Times* bestselling author. He is the writer, producer, and host of four successful public television programs, raising more than 20 million dollars for public television. He is a Distinguished Fellow of the American Psychiatric Association and the CEO and medical director of Amen Clinics in Newport Beach and Fairfield, California; Tacoma, Washington; and Reston, Virginia. Amen Clinics is the world leader in applying brain-imaging science to everyday clinical practice and has the world's largest database of functional scans related to behavior, now totaling more than 55,000.

Dr. Amen is the author of 35 professional scientific articles and 24 books, including *Change Your Brain, Change Your Body*, and the *New York Times* bestsellers, *Change Your Brain, Change Your Life* and *Magnificent Mind At Any Age*. He is also the author of *Healing ADD, Healing the Hardware of the Soul*, *Making a Good Brain Great*, *The Brain In Love*, and the co-author of *Healing Anxiety And Depression* and *Preventing Alzheimer's*.

Dr. Amen has appeared on the Dr. Oz Show, the Today Show, Good Morning America, The View, Larry King, The Early Show, CNN, HBO, Discovery Channel, and many other national television and radio programs. His national public television shows include Change Your Brain, Change Your Life; Magnificent Mind At Any Age; The Brain In Love; and Change Your Brain, Change Your Body.

A small sample of the organizations Dr. Amen has spoken for include: the National Security Agency (NSA), the National Science Foundation (NSF), Harvard's Learning and the Brain Conference, The Million Dollar Roundtable, Retired NFL Players Summit, and the Supreme Courts of Delaware, Ohio and Wyoming. Dr. Amen has been featured in *Newsweek, Parade Magazine*, the *New York Times Magazine, Men's Health,* and *Cosmopolitan*. Newsmax publishes Dr. Amen's monthly newsletter.

Dr. Amen is married to Tana, the father of four children, grandfather to Elias, and is an avid table tennis player.

AMEN CLINICS, INC.

Amen Clinics, Inc. (ACI) was established in 1989 by Daniel G. Amen, MD. They specialize in innovative diagnosis and treatment planning for a wide variety of behavioral, learning, emotional and cognitive, and weight problems for children, teenagers, and adults. ACI has an international reputation for evaluating brain-behavior problems, such as attention deficit disorder (ADD), depression, anxiety, school failure, brain trauma, obsessive-compulsive disorders, aggressiveness, marital conflict, cognitive decline, brain toxicity from drugs or alcohol, and obesity. Brain SPECT imaging is performed in the Clinics. ACI has the world's largest database of brain scans for behavioral problems.

ACI welcomes referrals from physicians, psychologists, social workers, marriage and family therapists, drug and alcohol counselors, and individual clients. We have clinics in:

Southern California
4019 Westerly Place #100
Newport Beach, CA 92660

Northern California
350 Chadbourne Road
Fairfield, CA 94534

Seattle Area
3315 S. 23rd street
Suite # 102
Tacoma, WA 98405

Washington DC, Area
1875 Campus Commons Dr.
Suite #101
Reston, VA 20191

Visit **www.amenclinics.com** or call 888-564-2700 for a consultation

Amenclinics.com is an educational interactive brain website geared toward mental health and medical professionals, educators, students, and the general public. It contains a wealth of information to help you learn about our clinics and the brain. The site contains over 300 color brain SPECT images, thousands of scientific abstracts on brain SPECT imaging for psychiatry, a brain puzzle, and much, much more.

View over 300 astonishing color 3-D brain SPECT images on:
Aggression • Attention Deficit Disorder, including the six subtypes • Dementia and cognitive decline • Drug Abuse • PMS • Anxiety Disorders • Brain Trauma • Depression Obsessive Compulsive Disorder • Stroke • Seizures